DESTINA
NC500

North Coast 500
CASTLES, BEACHES, AND SCOTTISH TRANQUILITY

Gemma Spence and Campbell Kerr
Destination Earth Guides

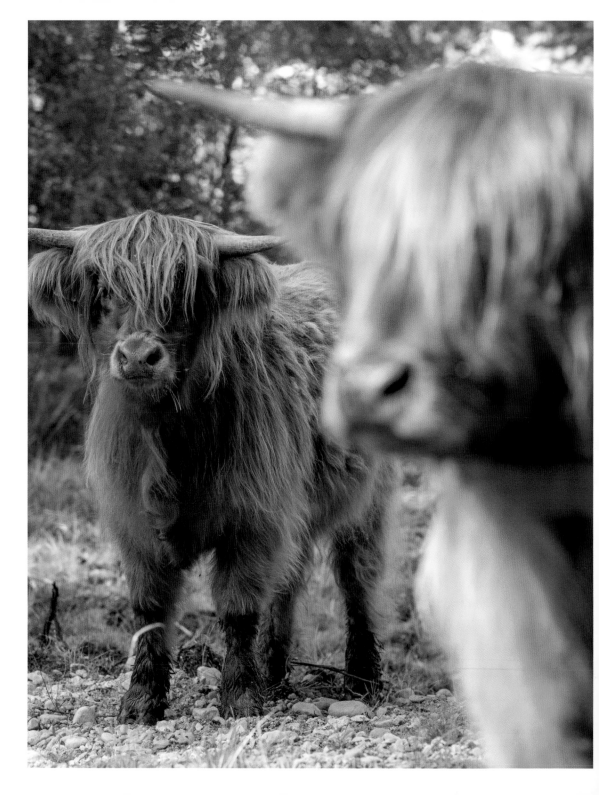

FOREWORD

As the old saying goes, "distance only makes the heart grow fonder".

After years of dreaming and planning, Gemma and I finally set off into the unknown when we left our bonnie homeland of Scotland behind on our round-the-world backpacking trip in 2018. We had always loved life in Scotland, but couldn't shake the feeling that we were missing something elsewhere in the world, an undiscovered beauty that couldn't be found in the highlands of our own backgarden.

What we found on this trip took us both by surprise, as despite all of the incredible mountains, crashing waterfalls, jungle retreats, fascinating wildlife, and delicious food that we discovered on our trip across the globe, none of it compared to what we had waiting for us back home. However, far from being a wasted journey, the adventure that lead to this epiphany ignited a passion in our hearts like we had never experienced before; the passion for storytelling.

On our return to our home country of Scotland, we were equipped with the knowledge and burning desire to show the beauty that Scotland has to behold to the world in greater detail that it has ever been done before. Combining the photography and travel-writing skills that we had developed over the years, we set off in our motorhome to spend the next three months in the highlands of Scotland, experiencing it in a way that only the luckiest have been able to enjoy.

The result of this 3-month expedition provided us with the experience necessary to produce the detailed and relatable travel guide on the North Coast 500 that you behold today. It is a guide that reflects the passion and dedication to the exploration of the Scottish highlands that we hold so dear, as well the appreciation and awareness that is necessary for its protection, to allow all future generations to enjoy it as we have.

We hope that this book proves useful to you not only in planning your own NC500 adventure, but in understanding what the beauty that you will find along the route means to the locals that you meet as you go.

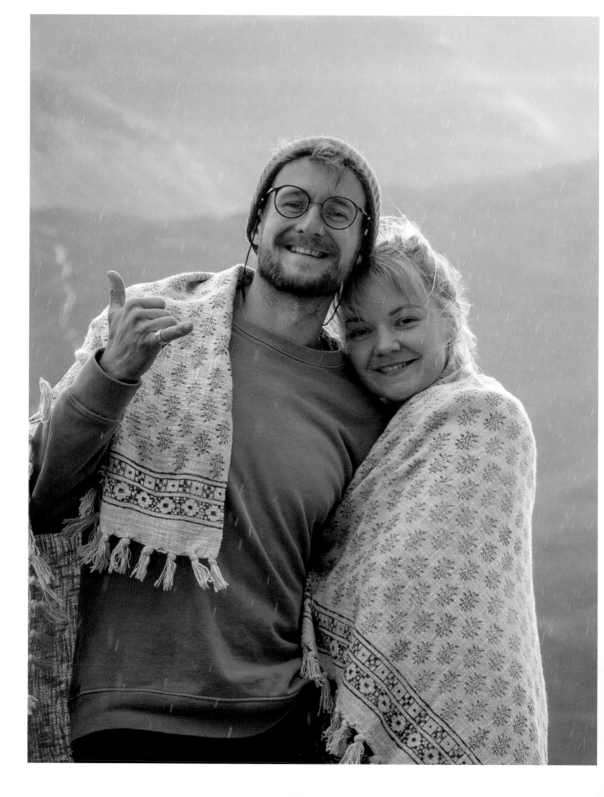

ABOUT THE AUTHORS

We are Gemma and Campbell, two Scots with a passion for adventure, the outdoors, alternative living, and being very cold (apparently..). In 2018, we quit our full time work in engineering and healthcare and set off with backpacks and no clue what life would bring, apart from assured disaster.

Over the next three years we would spend 5 months sleeping in a tent, before flying to Australia for 12 months to work on an olive farm for 3 months, live in a self-converted campervan for 6 months, before returning to live and work through the events of 2020 on the small island of Guernsey.

In 2021, we packed up our lives again and headed home to Scotland to travel in a van once again, this time turning over every leaf, stone and "highland coo" that we could find in order to ensure we did not miss a single thing from this guide.

This book is the product of the year of 2021, a year filled with late nights, early mornings, tears, laughter, blood and sweat, and a whole lot of unforgettable memories. We spent countless hours putting together the most in-depth guide to the North Coast 500 on the market so that you can truly make the most of your trip to Scotland, our bonnie home.

Instagram - @highlands2hammocks
Youtube - Highlands2hammocks

CONTENTS

SUMMARY OF NORTH COAST 500 ROUTE

Caithness

North West Sutherland

South East Sutherland

Easter Ross

Wester Ross

Black Isle

Inverness Shire

Scan the barcode here for access to the Destination NC500 map, showing all sights listed in this book

SCAN ME

INTRODUCTION

The NC500 is a 500mile (516 miles to be precise) circular road trip around the north of Scotland offering Caribbean-like beaches, raw and rugged mountains, and generally stunning scenery unique to this ancient part of the world.

The roads around the northern coast of the country have been in place for decades, however, branding of the North Coast 500 road trip in 2015 caused an explosion in popularity for this isolated part of Scotland.

This new official road trip provided a huge increase in awareness and opportunity for the smaller rural areas in the northern region of Scotland, creating hundreds of jobs. The aim was to encourage tourists to explore this beautiful part of the country and make it easier for them to plan their trips to the north of Scotland. The success of this initiative has seen the NC500 become busier year upon year, particularly in the warmer summer months, and it is not hard to see why.

In this book we share with you our expansive knowledge of this popular road trip, including the best sights to see, the most comfortable places to stay, and many, many more hints and tips to make your road trip around this beautiful part of our home country as smooth and enjoyable as possible.

Whether you are reading this having already set off on your road trip or are at home planning it, sit back, relax and enjoy the ride.

12 BLACK MUIR WOODS

4

What is the North Coast 500?

Beginning and ending in the northern capital of Inverness, the 516 mile road trip of the North Coast 500 takes you through some of the most breathtaking, ancient and formidable parts of the vast Scottish landscape.

Widely described as one of the most beautiful road trips in the world, the North Coast 500 offers the friendliest of welcomes to guests from across the globe every year, and boasts delicious food, comfortable accommodation, and unique holiday experiences that you will not find anywhere else on Earth. In 2015, the route was named one of the "Top 5 Coastal Routes in the World" by Now Travel Magazine, due to its beautiful scenery.

This chapter will give you a brief overview of the North Coast 500 road trip, including its fascinating history, the beautiful wildlife that can be seen along the route, why it is so popular, and what it means to us.

54 COLDBACKIE BEACH

56 CASTLE VARICH

6

History of the Region

The country of Scotland has an ancient and fascinating history, stretching back millions of years, when geographical events carved the dramatic landscape that we see today with massive tectonic shifts and glacial movements. Evidence of life in Scotland dates back 8,500 years prior to the start of Britain's recorded history, as early as 12,000BC. This can be found near Biggar on the Scottish Borders in the form of a hunter-gatherer encampment, a truly fascinating example of the rich history that Scotland has to behold.

Throughout this time, Scotland has experienced a turbulent history of fighting and expansion, from the invasion of the Vikings, to the formation of the Roman Empire. This continued all the way through the Scottish Wars of Independence, the Jacobite Uprising, and the explosion of Industrialism that saw Scotland become one of the leading ship-building centres of the world, and the city of Glasgow one of the largest cities on Earth.

56 CASTLE VARICH

It is due to this extraordinary concentration of world events in such a small country that gives Scotland the incredible depth and variety of historical sights that you can find today.

The northern region of Scotland, commonly referred to as the Highlands of Scotland, has an equally fascinating share of the country's history, mainly focused on the fishing and agricultural aspects of Highland life throughout the centuries. Due to the lack of urban development in this region, historical buildings are also in abundance all across the Highlands, with over 71 castles spread across the 10,000 sq miles of wilderness.

It is this history that makes the North Coast 500 road trip such a unique and special part of the world. Not only does this epic tour of Scotland offer stunning, natural views, but it also provides a fascinating insight into what life was like thousands of years ago.

Wildlife on the North Coast 500

From the hairy Highland Cows, to the leaping salmon of Lairg, the North Coast 500 is awash with beautiful and fascinating wildlife. All along the route you will have the opportunity to spot incredible native animals in their natural habitat, as well as some local favourites, such as the world-famous "hairy coo".

In terms of winged beasts, there are plenty of wild birds to be spotted along the NC500 route, so keep your eyes to the sky. Popular sightings include red kites, puffins, and golden eagles. Four-legged beasts include goats, red deer, and highland cows, and looking out to sea it is very likely that you may see dolphins, seals, and even whales and orcas.

We highly recommend bringing a set of binoculars and a camera with a good zoom for your road trip in Scotland, as you will most likely need it at some point.

Popularity of the North Coast 500

The North Coast 500 road trip itself was launched in 2015 by the North Highland Initiative tourism board, with the intention of developing and improving the tourism industry in a relatively untouched part of Scotland. The road trip was a huge success, with over 29,000 visitors in its first official year, resulting in an increase in expenditure in the region of over £9million. Since then the road trip has grown year upon year, becoming one of the most popular areas to visit in all of the UK.

This huge increase in popularity has led to some unexpected issues in the remote highlands of Scotland, involving a lack of infrastructure to be able to handle such a large influx of people and vehicles. Soil erosion, unmanageable littering, and over population of tourists are just some of the problems created by the North Coast 500's incredible growth.

In recent years, this has resulted in the road trip facing a backlash from locals along the route who are unhappy with the efforts that are being made to preserve the current landscape.

Despite these issues, it is still possible to visit the North Coast 500 responsibly and ensure that this beautiful road trip has a sustainable future. We will discuss our ideas and tips for visiting the North Coast 500 responsibly later in this guide.

52 FARR BEACH

50 STRATHY BEACH

88 SUILVEN

12

80 ACHMELVICH BEACH

Alternative Road Trips

With the North Coast 500 road trip proving such a huge success, the tourism boards around Scotland have been eagerly trying to promote similar ideas in other areas of the country in an attempt to spread the volume of tourism evenly across the land.

In addition to the highland circuit of the NC500, other up and coming road trips around Scotland include the newly launched Heart 200 road trip; the coastal routes around Fife, Angus and Argyle, the South West 300; Aberdeenshire's answer to the NC500, the North East 250; and of course, the incredible Isle of Skye road trip.

All of these road trips will show you a unique perspective of the beautiful scenery, culture, and history of Scotland, and are not to be overlooked in place of the NC500. Once you have completed the North Coast 500 road trip we highly recommend you check out these other routes as well.

95 ULLAPOOL

WHAT TO EXPECT

The NC500 is an exceptional experience. It is often reffered to as "Scotland's Route 66", however, we believe it cannot be compared. The scenery in this part of the world is jaw-dropping and unique, changing instantly from golden, sandy beaches and crystal clear water to towering mountains and deep, mystical lochs.

Roads
on the NC500

You will want to be an experienced driver to take on the roads around the NC500 as many of them are single track and extremely narrow and winding. Whilst navigating the blind corners and hairpin bends on these narrow roads, you also need to be prepared for sheep or deer who use the roads to get around.

In Scotland, we drive on the left and this is still the case on the single track roads. This can be very confusing/hazardous when moving between dual/single track roads, and it has been recommended by the local police to wear a band/bracelet on your left wrist as a reminder of which side you should be on.

Passing places are used to allow traffic to pass on the single track roads, it is important to remember that these are passing places and not parking places. When driving on these roads, keep a "passing place" distance apart from the cars in front of you to avoid congestion and pull in at the space at the side of the road to allow the oncoming traffic to pass you.

When it comes to the North Coast 500 driving the route is half of the fun, with stunning coastal views, breathtaking mountain ranges and beautiful wildlife to look out for. With all of this beauty to take in, it is especially important that you TAKE YOUR TIME.

Allow yourself to truly soak up the beauty of the land around you, coming to terms with how lucky we are to witness this paradise, rather than driving the NC500 to simply to get it over with.

A major cause of accidents and deaths in this part of the world is the result of distraction and haste, as people do not pay attention to the winding, narrow single track roads and rush between spots to see as much as possible. The best way to stay safe is to follow the road safety guidelines, drive slowly and don't rush - ENJOY.

The NC500's western side, in particular, is narrow and winding in stages, allowing access for one car at a time in some places to pass. This is part of the culture in this part of the world and by giving way to those passing, you will always be rewarded with a smile and a wave from a local, so do the right thing!

Follow the outdoor access code and park appropriately to maintain safety on the roads.

There have been a LOT of issues with passing places in recent years with people parking in these places and preventing the flow of traffic. When you are driving the narrow, beautiful roads and see a sight you want to stop and check out, DO NOT park in passing places.

Shops and Fuel
on the NC500

As for buying food and supplies around the NC500, choosing the right location to shop will save you a LOT of money during your trip. There are a number of large, cheap shops spread along the route, in between which you will find smaller, local shops.

Rather than finding yourself short along the route, the alternative is to stock up in Inverness with tinned and dried food, as well as plenty of snacks for the road trip. This will mean you can save your money for the huge variety of delicious local bars and restaurants that you will visit along the NC500.

The main shops that you want to aim for are Morrisons, Tesco, Aldi and Asda, most of which are located on the Southwestern part of the NC500. Once you head north of Dornoch you will only pass two more Tesco superstores, one in Wick and one at the end of the trip in Ullapool.

Petrol stations are quite evenly spread out along the NC500, however, you should know where each of them are and the distance between them to avoid running out of fuel on the road. To the right is a list of each of the petrol stations on the NC500 going counter-clockwise along the route.

Fuel stops along the route

- *Inverness* (distance to next – 15miles)
- *Dingwall* (distance to next – 24miles)
- *Tain* (distance to next – 23miles)
- *Brora* (distance to next – 46miles)
- *Wick* (distance to next – 16miles)
- *John O'Groats* (distance to next – 20miles)
- *Thurso* (distance to next – 30miles)
- *Bettyhill* (distance to next – 40miles)
- *Sango Sands* (distance to next – 25miles)
- *Scourie* (distance to next – 53miles)
- *Lochinver* (distance to next – 37miles)
- *Ullapool* (distance to next – 56miles)
- *Kinlochewe* (distance to next – 37/42miles)
- *Applecross* (distance to next – 17miles)
- *Lochcarron* (distance to next – 43miles)
- *Contin* (distance to next – 21miles)
- *Inverness*

Phone Reception
on the NC500

As you may have guessed, phone reception is very scarce throughout the majority of the North Coast 500. The best networks for signal along Scotland's northern coast and the more remote parts of the country are reportedly EE and Vodafone. Although phone signal is not guaranteed along the entire length of the NC500, you can expect to get good coverage on these networks for the majority of your trip.

Personally, on our trip in 2021 we used both Vodafone and Three, which provided us with signal on one or the other almost all of the time. If you are in desperate need of internet then the nearest town is always the best bet for any searching and downloading before you head off on your way again.

In order to prepare for this trip and the lack of cell reception, we highly recommend you download Google Maps to work offline for the area of the NC500. This will mean you can follow the directions from spot to spot without getting lost or relying on mobile data.

We also recommend either downloading your favourite music playlists or even go "old-school" with a good old CD player!

Weather
on the NC500

It is no secret that the weather in Scotland is a rather fickle thing. On average, the wettest parts of Scotland experience 5 rainy days a week, whilst the driest experience 3 days a week. This means that choosing the right time for a road trip as epic as the NC500 requires some care and consideration.

As a general rule of thumb, the months of the year that experience the best weather in Scotland are April, May and June. These months tend to be drier, with cooler mornings and clearer skies than later in summer. As the summer months go on, the humidity returns to the air and the rainfall begins once again, with July and August tending to be much wetter.

The additional perk of the early summer months is that (especially in April) the biting insects that are known as "midges" have not yet woken up. These bugs tend to come out when the warm rain begins and they have lots of water to lay their eggs in.

It might seem crazy to base an entire trip on the absence of some bugs, however, midges are a fierce, formidable force in the highlands, that have driven the hardiest of souls to tears.

How Long to Spend
on the NC500

This is one of the most common questions about the North Coast 500 when it comes to planning the road trip, however, it is one without a real answer (unfortunately). The basic answer is "it can take however long you want it to".

There are people who race around the NC500 in one day, making the most of the beautiful scenery, winding roads and white-knuckle driving conditions in certain areas. There are also people who slow travel around the NC500 for months at a time, making the most of every beach and soaking up the history at every stop.

How long SHOULD you spend on the NC500 is the better question to ask, and to that my answer is between 7-14 days.

When we first set off on the North Coast 500, we spent a total of 8 days on the coastal route. We found this to be enough time to see all of the best sights on the NC500, however, we could have easily spent more time at some of the beaches and mountain ranges to really explore them properly.

Given that the NC500 is one of the best roadtrips in the UK, I would suggest that you do not attempt the entire NC500 route in less than 7 days, otherwise, you won't be able to properly appreciate the beauty and fascinating history it has to behold.

Don't let this put you off, however, as if you do not have 7 days, you can still do PART of the NC500 on your trip to Scotland. For this we would we highly recommend you visit the western coast of the NC500, if nothing else.

In our opinion, the west is where the most spectacular scenery sits, with the dramatic hills and dreamy beaches. As the saying in Scotland goes, "West is Best", however, that is coming from two people who were born and raised in Glasgow, which could leave us being accused of being slightly biased.

THE WILDER SIDE OF LIFE

Perched at the edge of the world, the towering cliffs cascade waterfalls into the crashing sea below, while winds whistle across virgin sands, glinting and dancing with the glimour of the crystal-clear water that washes up along its deserted beaches. The northern coast of Scotland is a place like no other in this world.

It does not get much wilder than the North Coast 500 in Scotland, from the towering Munros that guard the coastline to the tempting glimour of the icy cold water of the North Sea. Escape from the tethers of modern day life, the restriction of the four-walls and a weekend, and head north to the wilderness and seclusion that awaits.

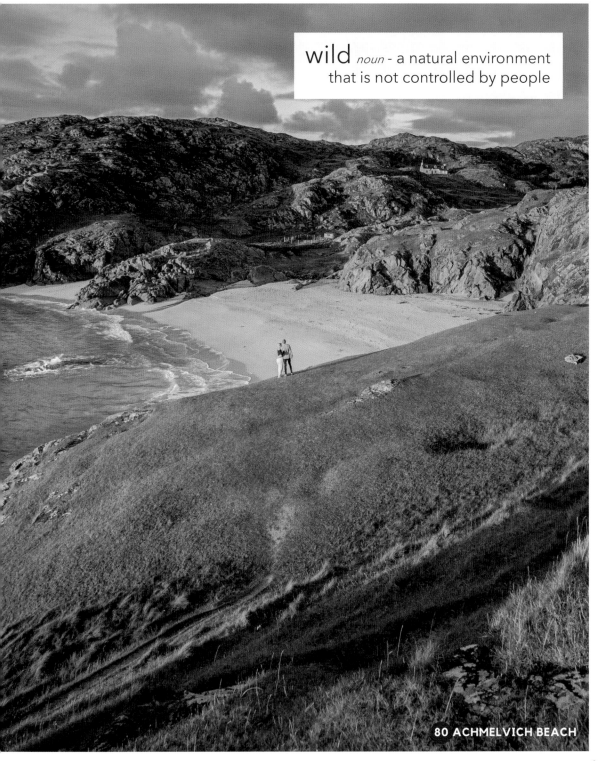

wild *noun* - a natural environment that is not controlled by people

80 ACHMELVICH BEACH

26

Wild Camping

One of Scotland's greatest charms is the Right to Roam law, allowing all persons to venture where you please, as long as you do so respectfully. The Land Reform (Scotland) Act 2003 allows wild camping in Scotland opening the door to the glorious and desolate highlands that Scotland has to offer, and the beauty that lies there. There is honestly no better feeling than getting out into the open and being the only one for miles around.

There is a positive tolerance and understanding from the locals when it comes to wild camping in Scotland, that may be due to the understanding that it brings tourism and business. However, when you are looking for a spot to pitch up for the night, you cannot just choose anywhere you wish. Some people might not take too kindly to waking up to discover you pitched up in their back garden.

24 DORNOCH BEACH

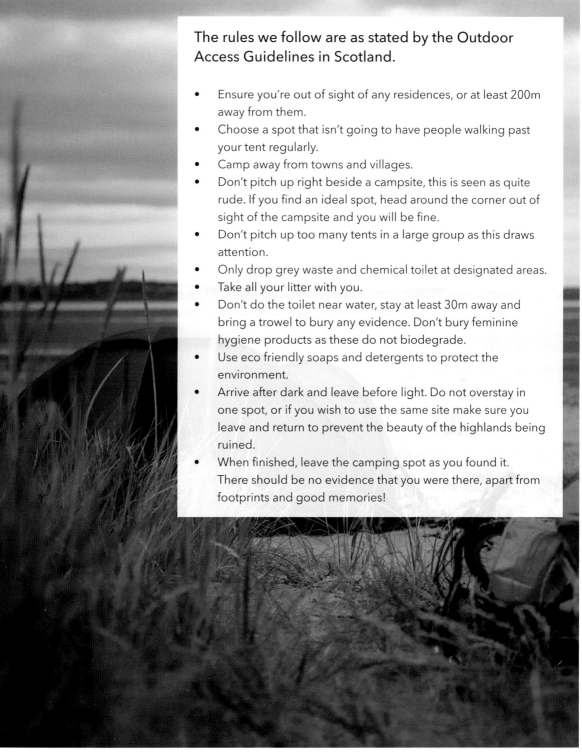

The rules we follow are as stated by the Outdoor Access Guidelines in Scotland.

- Ensure you're out of sight of any residences, or at least 200m away from them.
- Choose a spot that isn't going to have people walking past your tent regularly.
- Camp away from towns and villages.
- Don't pitch up right beside a campsite, this is seen as quite rude. If you find an ideal spot, head around the corner out of sight of the campsite and you will be fine.
- Don't pitch up too many tents in a large group as this draws attention.
- Only drop grey waste and chemical toilet at designated areas.
- Take all your litter with you.
- Don't do the toilet near water, stay at least 30m away and bring a trowel to bury any evidence. Don't bury feminine hygiene products as these do not biodegrade.
- Use eco friendly soaps and detergents to protect the environment.
- Arrive after dark and leave before light. Do not overstay in one spot, or if you wish to use the same site make sure you leave and return to prevent the beauty of the highlands being ruined.
- When finished, leave the camping spot as you found it. There should be no evidence that you were there, apart from footprints and good memories!

Highland Bothies

When it comes to life on the wild side, the bothies of Scotland are about as wild as it gets. Nestled among the towering peaks of the Scottish Highlands surrounded by vast wilderness with nothing but the howling of the wind to keep you company, sleeping in a bothy is perhaps one of the most unique experiences you will have in Scotland.

For those who have not heard of the term Bothy before, a Scottish Bothy is a small house (or hut) that sits in the most remote parts of the country. Once these huts would have been used as houses for farmers and shepherds, however, they have since fallen into ruin and been restored to a basic yet comfortable windproof and waterproof standard.

The idea behind the Scottish Bothy is to provide free shelter amongst one of the most dangerous and unforgiving environments on the planet. The huts are left unlocked and available for anyone and everyone to use as a place to rest for the night, sheltered from the harsh elements of the Scottish Highlands.

Bothies can be found across the length of Scotland, as well as in Wales and England, the vast majority of which are owned and maintained by the Mountain Bothy Association (MBA). This charity is responsible for the repair and upkeep of 97 bothies across the UK and is run by volunteers who love the wild side of the country so much they spend their weekends hiking across the land with the materials needed for the routine maintenance of the bothies.

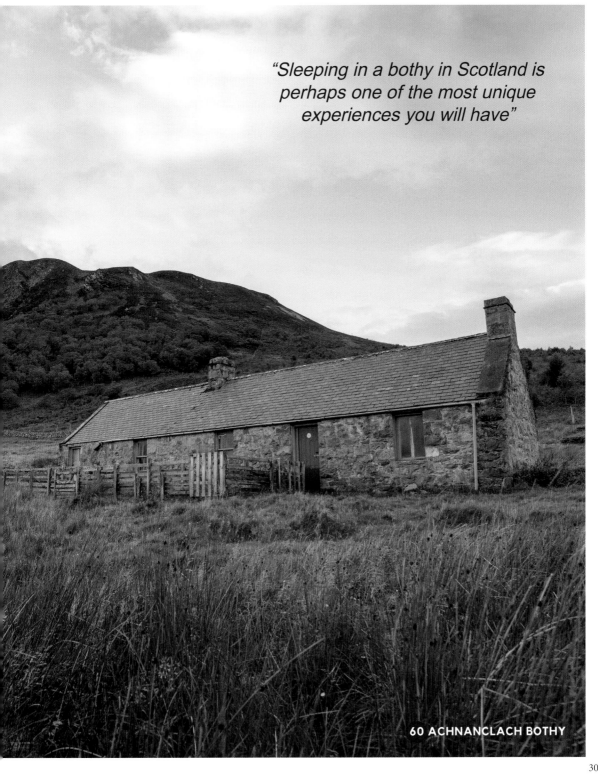

"Sleeping in a bothy in Scotland is perhaps one of the most unique experiences you will have"

60 ACHNANCLACH BOTHY

Over the years, the MBA have come up with a set of guidelines for the use of Mountain Bothies that ensure the continued enjoyment and use of bothies for years to come.

- Bothies are used entirely at your own risk.
- Leave the bothy clean and tidy with dry kindling for the next visitors.
- Make other visitors welcome.
- Report any damage to whoever maintains the bothy.
- Avoid burying rubbish; this pollutes the environment.
- If there is no toilet at the bothy please bury human waste out of sight and well away from the water supply; never use the vicinity of the bothy as a toilet.
- Never cut live wood or damage estate property. Use fuel sparingly.
- Large groups and long stays are to be discouraged – bothies are intended for small groups on the move in the mountains.
- Because of overcrowding and lack of facilities, large groups (6 or more) should not use a bothy nor camp near a bothy without first seeking permission from the owner. Bothies are not available for commercial groups.

IMPORTANT NOTE – If you do plan on using a bothy, research the season availability of the bothies in each area. During specific seasons, such as the Grouse Shooting and Stag Stalking season of September to October, access restrictions to the mountains/estates in certain areas do apply.

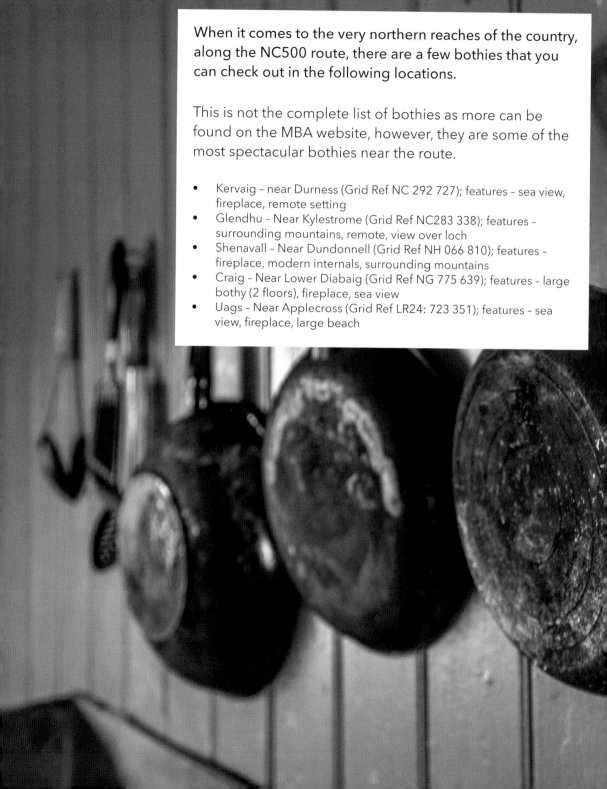

When it comes to the very northern reaches of the country, along the NC500 route, there are a few bothies that you can check out in the following locations.

This is not the complete list of bothies as more can be found on the MBA website, however, they are some of the most spectacular bothies near the route.

- Kervaig – near Durness (Grid Ref NC 292 727); features – sea view, fireplace, remote setting
- Glendhu – Near Kylestrome (Grid Ref NC283 338); features – surrounding mountains, remote, view over loch
- Shenavall – Near Dundonnell (Grid Ref NH 066 810); features – fireplace, modern internals, surrounding mountains
- Craig – Near Lower Diabaig (Grid Ref NG 775 639); features – large bothy (2 floors), fireplace, sea view
- Uags – Near Applecross (Grid Ref LR24: 723 351); features – sea view, fireplace, large beach

Please be aware that you will do this at your own risk. There are no lifeguards on the beaches or pools in the north of Scotland and the cold temperature means that hypothermia is a real risk. Research how to swim safely, always swim with a partner, and take a flotation aid with you.

Wild Swimming

There is something about wild swimming that gives us that sense of freedom and adventure. As our skin burns in the icy cold water we feel alive and ready to face whatever life throws at us. You can expect wild swimming in the north of Scotland to be cold, but that's where the excitement lies. The cold water actually makes your body feel relaxed and soothes muscle aches. It has also been known to boost your immune system.

It is safer to go swimming with a partner and not to stay in until you start shivering, as this means hypothermia has started to set in. Also make sure you have warm layers to put on when you get out. We would also recommend taking a hot water bottle or hot drink with you to heat up as soon as you get out of the water, as hypothermia is a serious risk when wild swimming in Scotland.

22 EMBO BEACH

Safety When Swimming

Ever-growing in popularity, wild swimming is uncovering a number of important safety factors that until recently have been generally overlooked here in Scotland. These involve the dangers of rip-currents, cold-shock, and after drop.

In order to stay safe whilst wild swimming, it is important to familiarise yourself with these terms, as well as the most effective ways to combat these dangers, which, if left untreated, can lead to fatal consequences.

Rip-currents - More applicable to seaside swimming, rip-currents refer to the pull of the tide leaving the shoreline between the swells that bring waves to the shore. Once caught in a rip-current, it can become very difficult, if not impossible, to swim against the flow of water that pulls you out to sea. In order to get out of the current, it is necessary to swim parallel to the shoreline (with the shore on your left/right) until you are out of the rip and then swim into shore.

Cramps - Due to the extreme cold, cramps can be increasingly common when wild swimming, compared to a heated pool. If you experience cramp in your legs or arms, it is important not to panic and exert more energy. Your body is naturally buoyant, so utilise this advantage and call for help whilst lying on your back with your ears in the water. This will allow your body to balance and float with ease until you can be rescued or the cramp disappears.

Afterdrop - The continued decline of your internal body temperature after you leave the water. This can often be spotted by a delay in shivering once you have left the water and begin to get dressed. It is important to make sure that you do not wait until you begin to shiver before you leave the water, as this means that hypothermia has already begun to set in.

Cold-shock - The involuntary gasp and seizing of muscles that your body experiences when you enter cold water. This can have serious consequences if you dip your head beneath the water, as it can result in inhalation

Blood-rush - Once you have exited the water, the desire to hop straight into a hot shower can often be too great to resist. However, this can often prove to be a dangerous move as a lot of cold water swimmers often end up fainting in the shower. This is caused by the dialation (opening) of your blood vessels in your outer extremities due to the external heat of the water, which causes the cold blood that was in your arms and legs to rush back to your internal organs. This can often result in a huge and sudden drop in your body's internal temperature, which can lead to mild hypothermia and even death.

Hiking

Beaches and bothies aside, one of the most impressive parts of the NC500 route is the stark contrast of the towering mountains to the endless horizon, divided only by the road leading out before you.

The mountains around the NC500 are out of this world and will no doubt be a highlight of your trip around this wild and ever changing landscape. As beautiful as the views are from the bottom, it is well worth a hike up to see the views from the top.

From Corbetts to full-blown Munros, there is a huge variety of outdoor adventures just waiting for you to explore along this route.

14 BEN WYVIS

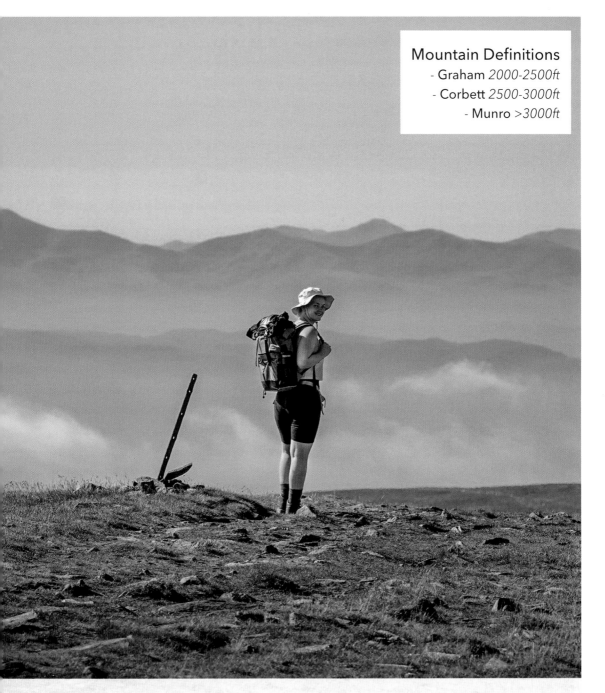

Mountain Definitions
- Graham *2000-2500ft*
- Corbett *2500-3000ft*
- Munro *>3000ft*

Please be aware that you will do this at your own risk. Hiking in Scotland can be a dangerous activity, with unpredictable weather systems and an isolated and remote countryside. Before you leave on any hike it is recommended that you pack for bad weather, bring a map and compass, and let someone know where you are going.

Wildlife

Due to the incredible size and remoteness of the Scottish Highlands the amount of wildlife that you are likely to see around the North Coast 500 is simply amazing. From the winged raptors such as the golden eagle soaring high over the mountain tops, to the highly intelligent and fun loving dolphins on the shores, and the iconic Scottish sight of the Hairy Coo, the NC500 has it all.

You will have multiple opportunities to find each of these beautiful creatures as you travel around the North Coast 500, so to help you plan your sightings on the right are some areas that you are most likely to spot wildlife along the route.

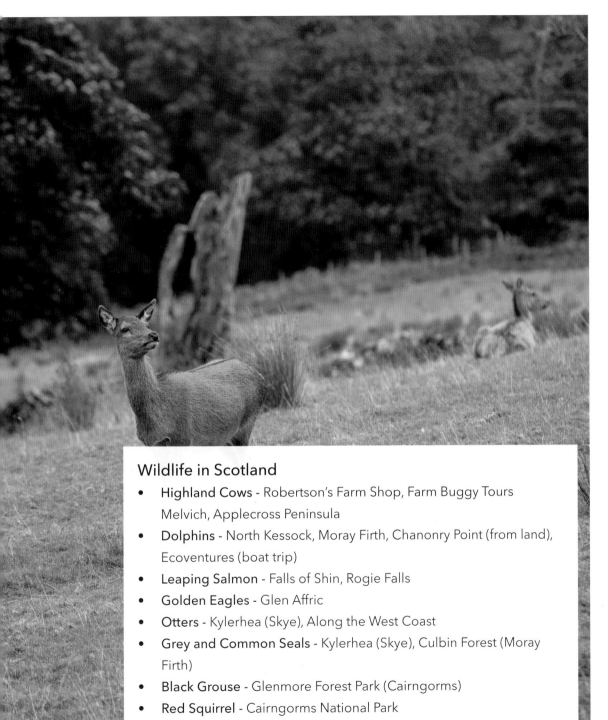

Wildlife in Scotland

- **Highland Cows** - Robertson's Farm Shop, Farm Buggy Tours Melvich, Applecross Peninsula
- **Dolphins** - North Kessock, Moray Firth, Chanonry Point (from land), Ecoventures (boat trip)
- **Leaping Salmon** - Falls of Shin, Rogie Falls
- **Golden Eagles** - Glen Affric
- **Otters** - Kylerhea (Skye), Along the West Coast
- **Grey and Common Seals** - Kylerhea (Skye), Culbin Forest (Moray Firth)
- **Black Grouse** - Glenmore Forest Park (Cairngorms)
- **Red Squirrel** - Cairngorms National Park
- **Red Deer** - Glen Affric, Cairngorms Ski Slope, any large forest area

Essential Guidelines for Wild Activities

- Only camp where it is acceptable.
- Do not disturb the surrounding area and respect the locals. Remember you are their guest, act as such.
- When you leave the area make sure you leave nothing but footprints and take nothing but memories! This is the biggest crime you can do while wild camping and is the main reason it is becoming illegal.
- Bury your waste (including the toilet paper, or carry a bag to dispose of it in). Don't leave your business lying around.
- Do not overstay your welcome. Arriving after dark and leaving before light will ensure that people can continue to use these areas without complaints.

Responsibly Wild

The most beautiful part of the highlands of Scotland comes with how remote, rugged, and unforgiving the environment can be. The wilderness of the northern region of the UK has remained barren and uninhabited for hundreds, if not, thousands of years, far from the reach of the modern society.

With the blessing of the remote and untamable wilderness that can be found along the North Coast 500 comes with great responsibility to the increasing number of tourists who explore the route. A responsibility to admire, respect, and protect the beauty of this natural landscape.

Across Scotland, there are more and more spaces where wild camping has been made illegal, mainly due to the disrespect shown by the small minority of those camping who have abused this luxury and destroyed the environment.

No matter what wild activity you wish to partake in, the key message remains the same.

Leave No Trace.

BEST OF THE NORTH COAST 500

In the modern day world of short attention spans and the constant urgency for the next destination, project, or story, perhaps what makes the North Coast 500 such an unforgettable experience is how easy it is to find yourself lost in the beauty and wonder of nature. Entirely removed from the stresses of modern-life, with no time-scale to follow, limited phone signal to keep you grounded, and sometimes hours of exploration with no contact with another living soul, the northern wilderness of Scotland is a different world to what we all consider "normality" in this digital age.

Yet, despite the deafening solitude that can be found all across this Highlands of Scotland, there is an unbelievable abundance of historical, cultural, gastronomical, and simply unmissable sights and attractions to be found along the NC500.

From the famous whisky distilleries that supply the world with liquid fire, to the ancient castles that populate this area of the country, lying in ruin or beautifully restored in splendour, the northern regions of the United Kingdom are full of sights that once visited, will stay with you for all eternity.

It is this part of Scotland that gives its visitors a final meaning and understanding to the poem, My Heart is in the Highlands.

My heart's in the Highlands, my heart is not here,
My heart's in the Highlands, a-chasing the deer;
Chasing the wild-deer, and following the roe,
My heart's in the Highlands, wherever I go.

- Robert Burns, 1789

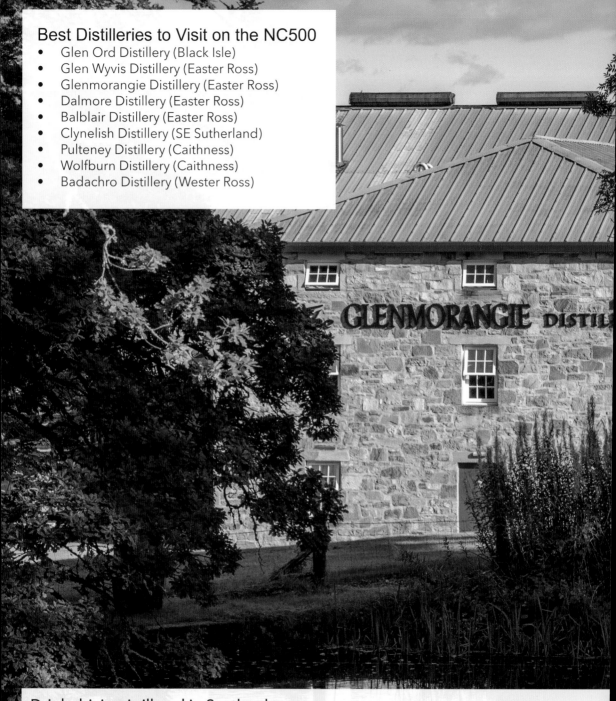

Best Distilleries to Visit on the NC500
- Glen Ord Distillery (Black Isle)
- Glen Wyvis Distillery (Easter Ross)
- Glenmorangie Distillery (Easter Ross)
- Dalmore Distillery (Easter Ross)
- Balblair Distillery (Easter Ross)
- Clynelish Distillery (SE Sutherland)
- Pulteney Distillery (Caithness)
- Wolfburn Distillery (Caithness)
- Badachro Distillery (Wester Ross)

Drink driving is illegal in Scotland. If you are driving around the North Coast 500 then it is important to highlight that NO ALCOHOL should be consumed before driving in Scotland. Due to the low legal limit in Scotland, it is also recommended that you wait 24hrs after drinking before driving.

Best Distilleries
on the NC500

Where better is there to sample a taste of Scotland's most famous product; the golden, fiery, and incredibly delicious Scotch Whisky? The highlands of Scotland are synonomous with the liquid fire that is known as whisky, and what better place is there for its production than in the mountainous terrain of the north, one of the wettest locations on earth.

Everything about the process of whisky production is fascinating to behold, from the rich and diverse history that each distillery has to tell, to the subtle changes in techniques, flavour, and focus that each Master Distiller imparts on the final product.

Whisky production dates back hundreds of years, beginning as a way for farmers to make a little more money on the side with the by-products of their main business. Eventually, the industry was legitimised and the rules for producing Single Malt Scotch Whiskey were set in stone; it must be produced using only malted barley, water, and yeast, and it must be aged in an oak cask for at least 3 years, then bottled at no less than 40% alcohol.

Despite these pretty solid guidelines for the production of whisky, the variety of flavours and textures of whisky that the different regions of Scotland produce are mind-blowing.

There is no better time to put this variety of flavours to the test than during the 500 mile road trip around Scotland's most northern distilleries. Many distilleries offer tours (either complimentary or paid) that provide a fascinating insight into the production of the specific whisky distilled at that location, and are usually rounded off with a tasting session for you to sample the final product.

Obviosuly, if you are driving then you will not be able to partake in this final tasting, however, fear not as a lot of distilleries offer sample kits to be taken away and enjoyed later in the evening instead.

Best Castles to Visit on the NC500
- Inverness Castle (Inverness-shire)
- Castle Leod (Easter Ross)
- Dunrobin Castle and Gardens (SE Sutherland)
- Castle of Old Wick (Caithness)
- Castle Sinclair and Girnigoe (Caithness)
- Old Keiss Castle (Caithness)
- Castle and Gardens of Mey (Caithness)
- Castle Varrich (NE Sutherland)
- Ardvreck Castle (NE Sutherland)
- Hermit's Castle (NE Sutherland)
- Strome Castle (Wester Ross)

Best Castles
on the NC500

An ancient, formidable, and seemingly forgotten part of the world, parts of the highlands of Scotland appear to have a distinct lack of any sign of modern-day society. This barren and desolate part of Scotland has remained largely uninhabited for centuries, driving off the unrelenting encroachment of civilisation on its wild lands with its extreme weather, terrain, and inacessability.

As a result of this lack of societal development, the historical sights and locations on Scotland's northern coast have survived and remain relatively untouched since their abandonment.

In addition to these various ruins of time, there are also a huge number of maintained castle buildings, some of which being restored to their former beauty, others having never been out of use.

At one point in time, the highlands of Scotland were host to over 70 historically significant buildings, making it one of the densest parts of the country for castle ruins.

It goes without saying, therefore, that any trip to the Highlands of Scotland must include a visit to at least one of these fascinating and fairytalesque buildings.

Whether you prefer a guided tour of the beautiful internals and grandure of a restored castle, or you would rather get down and dirty in the ancient remains of an abandoned castle ruin, the North Coast 500 has the perfect day out for you, just waiting to be explored.

37 CASTLE SINCLAIR AND GIRNIGOE

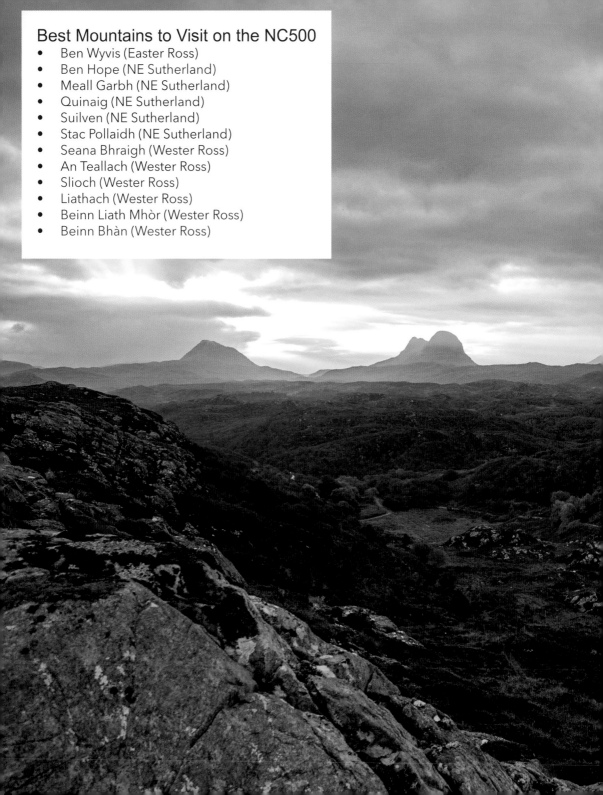

Best Mountains to Visit on the NC500

- Ben Wyvis (Easter Ross)
- Ben Hope (NE Sutherland)
- Meall Garbh (NE Sutherland)
- Quinaig (NE Sutherland)
- Suilven (NE Sutherland)
- Stac Pollaidh (NE Sutherland)
- Seana Bhraigh (Wester Ross)
- An Teallach (Wester Ross)
- Slioch (Wester Ross)
- Liathach (Wester Ross)
- Beinn Liath Mhòr (Wester Ross)
- Beinn Bhàn (Wester Ross)

Best Mountains
on the NC500

The story of Scotland's dramatic, beautiful and very iconic landscape began roughly 600 million years ago, when the northern regions of Scotland were all part of a different continent known as Laurentia. During this time, the land masses that are today known as Scotland and England were seperated by the Iapetus Ocean.

500 million years ago, continental forces drove these two sections of land together, closing up the Iapetus Ocean and eventually bringing about a series of continental collisions, now known as the Caledonian Mountain-building Event.

Fast forward a couple hundred million years, as the two continents ground against each other, thrusting layers of rock upwards, opening pockets in the crust for volcanoes, and forming the dramatic ridges that make up the Scottish Highlands that we see today. From there, it was Mother Nature that finished off the modern-day masterpiece that we admire today, with glacial movements carving out the deep glens, and the unrelenting weather systems smoothing out and wearing down the towering peaks.

88 SUILVEN

It is thanks to these unfathomably large events that gives rise to the incredible number of mountains that the north of the British Isles has to behold. Moving from east to west, the landscape becomes noticably more rugged and inhospitable, as the mountains and glens increase in number, size, and breathtaking beauty.

The sayings "good things take time", and "Rome wasn't built in a day" do not ring more true than when referring to the stunning landscapes of the Scottish Highlands. And here it all lies today, just waiting for you to explore this beautiful wilderness and discover the tranquility and peace that is unique to this ancient part of the world.

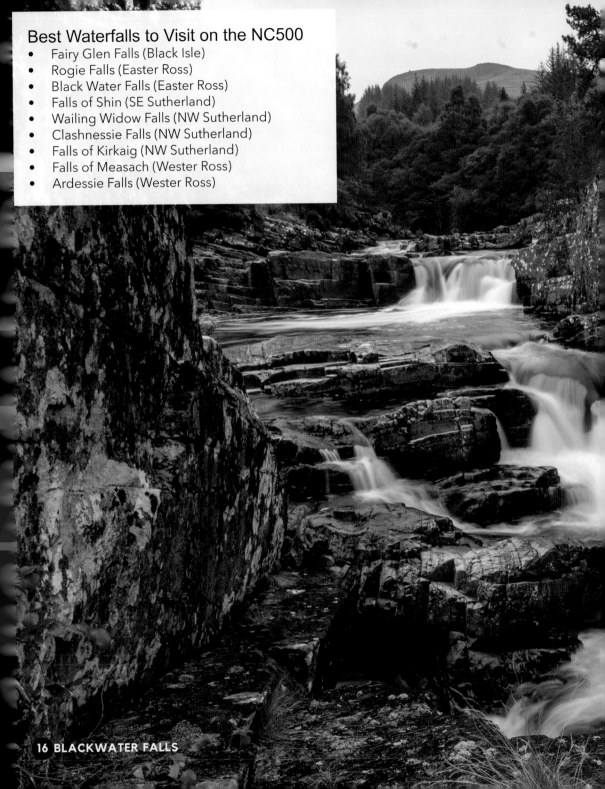

Best Waterfalls to Visit on the NC500

- Fairy Glen Falls (Black Isle)
- Rogie Falls (Easter Ross)
- Black Water Falls (Easter Ross)
- Falls of Shin (SE Sutherland)
- Wailing Widow Falls (NW Sutherland)
- Clashnessie Falls (NW Sutherland)
- Falls of Kirkaig (NW Sutherland)
- Falls of Measach (Wester Ross)
- Ardessie Falls (Wester Ross)

Best Waterfalls
on the NC500

The northern regions of the British Isles are famous throughout the world for the exceptionally high amount of rainfall that they experience every year. It is said that parts of the highlands of Scotland experience rainfall 2 out of every 3 days. This high level of rainfall makes Scotland one of the wettest regions in all of Europe, with up to 4500mm of rain annually.

However, this rather soggy characteristic gives life to the beautiful stretches of endless greenery that you can see here in Scotland, as well as the rarest rainforest habitats in the world. It is here that the last footholds of the Celtic Rainforest exist in the world, with as little as 30,000 hectares of the woodland left.

In addition to this natural wildlife, Scotland's extreme rain, combined with its dramatic landscape, means only one thing; Scotland is made for waterfalls.

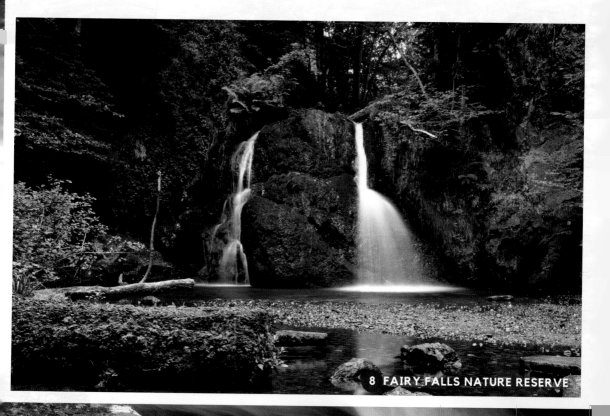

8 FAIRY FALLS NATURE RESERVE

Best Beaches to Visit on the NC500

- Dornoch Beach (SE Sutherland)
- Embo Beach (SE Sutherland)
- Reiss Beach (Caithness)
- Bay of Sannick (Caithness)
- Dunnet Bay (NW Sutherland)
- Coldbackie Sands (NW Sutherland)
- Ceannabiene Beach (NW Sutherland)
- Sango Sands Beach (NW Sutherland)
- Balnakeil Beach (NW Sutherland)
- Sandwood Bay (NW Sutherland)
- Oldshoremore Beach (NW Sutherland)
- Clachtoll Beach (NW Sutherland)
- Achmelvich Bay (NW Sutherland)
- Gruinard Beach (Wester Ross)
- Firemore Beach (Wester Ross)
- Big Sand Beach (Wester Ross)

Best Beaches
on the NC500

Stretching over 6000 miles in length, dancing in and out of the rugged scenery and twisting its way around the many islands that make up the North, the coastline of Scotland is as beautiful as it is dramatic. Between the towering cliffs and craggy shores, hidden beaches of white sand and torquoise blue water are dotted along the coast.

If someone were to blindfold you and lead you through the winding roads of the northern region, revealing to you the empty, golden beaches that Scotland has to offer, you would be hard pressed not to believe that you have travelled across the sea to the Carribean (until you dip your toe in the icy water that is...).

49 MELVICH BAY

The most beautiful beaches in the world can be found along the North Coast 500 route, tranquil and abandoned, and as peaceful as the mountains that overlook them. In fact, so great in number are they, that if you find a beach that is a little too busy for your liking, all you need to do is head to the next one to find your own slice of paradise.

The temperature of the sea at these beaches may not be that of the tropics, however, don't let that stop you from exploring and enjoying the beaches of Scotland during your road trip. Bring swimwear (and possibly a wetsuit), and see for yourself the clear water of Achmelvich and the stunning views above Ceannabeine beach.

62 BALNAKEIL BEACH

54 COLDBACKIE BEACH

INVERNESS-SHIRE

Through the beginnings of a wilderness that hints of the beauty and serenity that lies ahead, your road north along the famous A9 brings you to what is known as the capital of the highlands of Scotland, Inverness. This ancient part of the country has stood almost immune to the passing of time, as steadfast as the mountains that decorate its horizons and the moss covered stones that speckle the fields all around you.

The region of Inverness-shire spreads as far west as the southern isles of the Outer Hebrides, encompassing all of the land between there and the A9, including the misty islands of Skye. It is the second largest county out of the whole of the UK, despite being home to less than 2% of Scotland's population, evident by the sheer isolation that you can experience whilst venturing through its rugged terrain.

Meeting place and common ground of the highlands and lowlands of Scotland, this historical part of the country is home to many stories of Kings, Queens, battles, and bloodshed, from the famous flight of Bonnie Prince Charlie, to the haunting slaughter at the Battle of Culloden.

It is a place that, despite being only a taster of the wildness that lies ahead on the NC500, sparks an instinctive desire that we all feel when we see a wilderness stretched out before us; *the desire to explore.*

That being said, the vibrant, lively, and outstanding welcome of the city of Inverness may just be the reason why so many travellers have hurried to its gates throughout the centuries. This city offers a resolute and comfortable croft to any and all wanderers in need of respite before they continue into the rugged lands of the north and beyond.

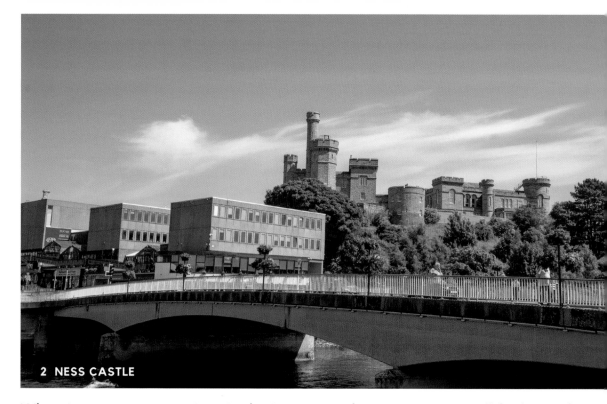

2 NESS CASTLE

When it comes to attractions in the Inverness-shire region, you will find a perfect balance between ancient and modern culture, stunning scenery and adrenaline-fuelled activities. The city of Inverness is the last notably large place that you will encounter on your trip through the highlands, and as such, it best to make the most of your time in this vibrant town before going on your way.

Visit the local whisky bars, enjoy the fantastic cuisine, and experience the local nightclubs to celebrate the start of your trip, however, don't stay up too late as you have a lot of exploring to do.

1. Inverness Cathedral

The most northerly cathedral in the country sits right in the centre of Scotland's capital of the north, Inverness. The Inverness Cathedral is a magnificent building built in 1866, which consists of two towers and a long hall decorated with beautiful mosaics and carvings.

This cathedral is free to enter all year round and offers a unique insight to the history of the Church of Scotland over the years. There is also a gift shop and cafe that serves delicious cakes near the cathedral that are both open 6 days a week.

-> *Inverness Cathedral can be found on the southern side of the River Ness, directly across from the towers of Ness Castle. The best places to park to visit this attraction, as well as the rest of the sights in Inverness town centre, are Cathedral Car Park or the Public Car Park at the northern end of the city.*

Inverness Castle

The main sight that you will not want to miss in the city centre of Inverness is the local castle. This grand building sits high above River Ness, unmistakable with its red sandstone walls. In order to reach the castle, head down the high street towards the river and take a left along the river bank.

Stop and enjoy the view here before walking along the river until the castle comes into sight. Although the original site dates back to the 11th century, the structure visible today was built in 1836. The grounds are open to the public, however, the rest of the castle is restricted as it houses the Inverness Justice Centre.

Inverness Castle sits high above the River Ness in the town centre of Inverness. It is only accessible by foot and car parking available at the Cathedral Car Park *or the* Public Car Park *at the northern end of the city.*

1 INVERNESS CATHEDRAL

3 CULLODEN BATTLEFIELD

3. Culloden Battlefield

To the east of Inverness lies one of the most infamous battlefields in the UK, the site of the Battle of Culloden. Thought to be the definitive battle that ended the Jacobite Uprising, this brutal clash of enemy forces saw over 1600 lives extinguished in just over one hour.

You can visit the battlefield and take a guided tour of the site, learning about the history and events that took place in this period of Scotland's history in vivid detail.

-> *The battlefield itself lies 15 minutes from Inverness by car, following the signposts and leaving the A9 onto the B9006 and follow the road until you arrive. Alternatively, you can catch the No.2 bus from the town centre of Inverness.*

Loch Ness

way from the civilisation of Inverness and the surrounding villages sits one of Scotland's ost famous attractions. Time your visit to the loch early on a cold morning, as the mist nd fog still clings to the top of the water, hiding the secrets of the dark, bottomless water nd all that it contains.

1e peace and tranquility that you can find at Loch Ness, especially if you choose to xplore the less-travelled eastern side of the loch, is simply magical.

Drive south on the A82 from Inverness and you will reach Lochend at the northern tip of Loch Ness in 15 minutes. :ernatively, you can catch the 919 bus.

4 LOCH NESS

5. Ness Islands

This is a collection of islands that sit in the centre of the River Ness. There is beautiful nature walks around the island which are connected by old Victorian style bridges. You can enter on one side of the island and exit from the other side. It is a lovely peaceful place to sit and watch the water flow by on the banks of River Ness.

-> *Follow the river East from Ness castle and you will arrive at the islands after 25 minutes.*

6. Leakey's Bookshop

Built in an old church, the interior is also unique with a winding staircase in the middle of the room taking you upstairs to the open plan second floor. It is considered to be the second largest second hand book store in Scotland with over 100,000 books.

-> *Located at the northern end of Church Street. Open Mon-Sat 10am-5pm.*

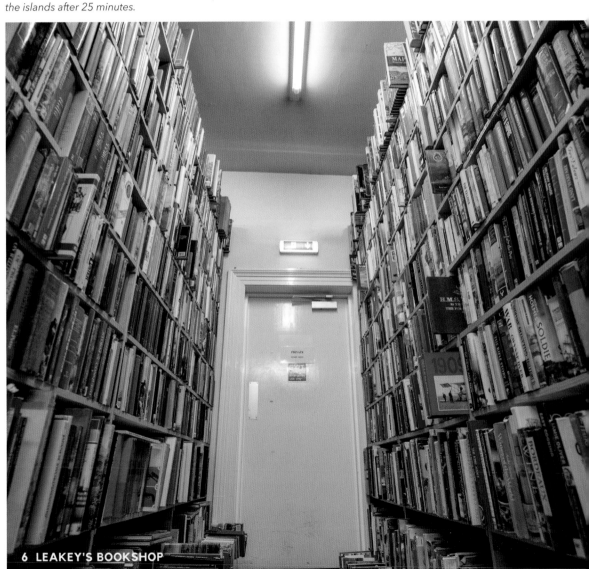

6 LEAKEY'S BOOKSHOP

Where to Eat
in Inverness

MacGregor's Bar
A cosy and classic pub filled with great atmosphere, seasonal dishes, local ingredients, and plenty of whisky to go round. This bar offers the perfect authentic highland bar experience.

-> 109-113 Academy St, Inverness IV1 1LX. Dog friendly.

The Castle Tavern
A locally-owned, real-ale bar offering wholesome and warming meals with a relaxing atmosphere. It also has a beer garden and a variety of ales for you to enjoy with a view of Ness Castle.

-> 1 View Pl, Inverness IV2 4SA

The Mustard Seed
Overlooking the River Ness, this is a cosy and picturesque restaurant offering a unique dining experience in an old, converted church building. One of Inverness's favourite dine-outs.

-> 16 Fraser St, Inverness IV1 1DW. Dog friendly.

The White House
A stark contrast to the aging stones and decorative archway that welcomes you inside, the White House is a modern and stylish cocktail bar, also offering great food and a good night out.

-> 50 Union St, Inverness IV1 1PX. Dog friendly.

Scotch and Rye
Visit 1920's America with this Scottish take on a Chicago Speakeasy gastropub, with everything from mouthwatering food to fresh beer and swanky cocktails.

-> 21 Queensgate, Inverness IV1 1DF. Dog friendly.

Oakwood Restaurant at Highland Lassie
It doesn't get much more unique than enjoying Scotland's finest seafood aboard a floating hotel. Local produce and vegetarian options make this a must visit.

-> Canal Side, Dochgarroch, Inverness IV3 8JG. Dog friendly.

Where to Stay
in Inverness

Hotels in Inverness
- River Ness Hotel
- Best Western Inverness Palace
- Jurys Inn Inverness
- The Royal Highland Hotel
- Mercure Inverness Hotel

Apartments in Inverness
- Waverly Inn Holiday Apartments
- Bridge Street Apartments
- Highland Apartments by Mansley
- Inverness City Suites

Campsites in Inverness

Torvean Caravan Park
Sitting southwest of Inverness on the banks of the Caledonian Canal, this park offers touring pitches, holiday lodges, and even motorhome rentals.

-> Glenurquhart Rd, Inverness IV3 8JL. Dog friendly.

Bught Park Caravan Park & Campsite
In the city centre of Inverness, Bught Park offers easy access to the main sights of Inverness, with pitches for tents, caravans and motorhomes.

-> Bught Ln, Inverness IV3 5SR. Dog friendly.

Ardtower Caravan Park
Situated nearby the famous Culloden Battlefield, this caravan park offers spectacular views of the Moray Firth below. Free wifi and all types of pitches available.

-> Culloden Rd, Westhill, Inverness IV2 5AA. Dog friendly.

Road Trip Essentials
Inverness

Food Shops
Asda
Aldi
Tesco Superstore
Iceland
B&M
Home Bargains
Lidl

Water Points
- Old Ticket Office Toilets
- Tore Service Station
- Dochgarroch Lock

Chemical Waste Disposal
- Highland Campervans
- Beauly Holiday Park

5 NESS ISLANDS

THE BLACK ISLE

As you soar high above the glass-like water of the Moray Firth, clouds and sky reflecting off its crystal surface, the road to the north begins its slow wind into the distant mountains of the highlands. The unmistakable outline of the Kessock bridge that frames the city of Inverness is the next stage of your North Coast 500 adventure, crossing over to the Black Isle of Ross and Cromarty.

Despite its name, the Black Isle is actually a peninsula, famous for its rich farmland, enchanting waterfalls, beautiful beaches, and local food and drink specialities. Its name dates back to the wilder times of Britain, when the peninsula was covered mostly in dark and dense woodland, some of which can still be found, tucked away across the isle.

8 FAIRY FALLS NATURE RESERVE

The Black Isle became a popular crossing point after the construction of the Kessock Bridge in 1982, drawing commuters and tourists alike to explore the quiet northern fishing towns of Avoch and Rosemarkie. The most famous sight on the peninsula is no doubt the vantage point of Chanonry Point, where it is not uncommon to see local wildlife such as dolphins, porpoises, and seals.

The Black Isle is also home to a number of culinary treats, such as the Black Isle Brewery, Scotland's only organic brewing company. Spend some time relaxing and unwinding on the peaceful beaches of the Black Isle, exploring the forests and nature reserves that the island has to behold, and make sure to time your visit to Chanonry Point so as to catch a glimpse of the beautiful sea creatures of Scotland.

7. Chanonry Point

Just to the north of Inverness, slightly off track and definitely off the beaten path, the small peninsula known as Chanonry Point is the best place in the Moray Firth for dolphin spotting.

If you want to get even closer to these magnificent creatures, there are a number of dolphin tours available from Inverness, including the Dolphin Spirit tours that leave from the north of the city on the east bank o the river.

-> *Follow the A832 north through the Black Isle until you reach the town of Fortrose, where you turn right onto Ness Road. Th road will lead through a golf course to the car park at the end. Parking here is free before 9am. You can also catch the 26A or 26C Stagecoach bus from Inverness, dropping you off in Fortrose where you will have a 30 minute walk to the lighthouse point.*

7 CHANONRY POINT

. Fairy Falls Nature Reserve

he Fairy Glen Falls is a beautiful waterfall located not far from the small town of osemarkie. The walk to reach the falls twists and turns through the overhang of the forest, reating a magical and fairytale-like setting for the waterfalls themselves.

he waterfalls will either be a trickling stream or a raging torrent, depending on how much ain you have been having. The second waterfall lies at the top of the first, following the teps to a wide open expanse of forest, where the waterfall tumbles down the rockface nto a still pool at the bottom.

Parking is either at the Fairy Falls car park on the A832 or on the seafront of Rosemarkie. The route will take you about 20 inutes from the car park and is fairly rough, muddy terrain, unsuitable for those with mobility impairments.

8 FAIRY FALLS NATURE RESERVE

9. Avoch Harbour

A quiet port on the banks of the Moray Forth, mainly used as a harbour for local fishing boats and sea tours. This is a beautifully peaceful point to park up and enjoy a stroll or picnic before heading further north.

-> A short drive off the A9 along the A832. Plenty of parking as it is not a popular stopping point.

10. Black Isle Brewing Co.

Scotland's first ever fully organic brewery, the Black Isle Brewery is paving the way for brewing across the globe. Opened in 1998, the owner, David Gladwin, aimed to produce a beer that did not rely on destructive chemicals to produce a delicious and refreshing beer. Today, over 10,000 litres are shipped around the globe from this tiny peninsula.

-> Located on the A832. Open Mon-Sun 10am-5pm. Daily tours available, contact for specific details and availability .

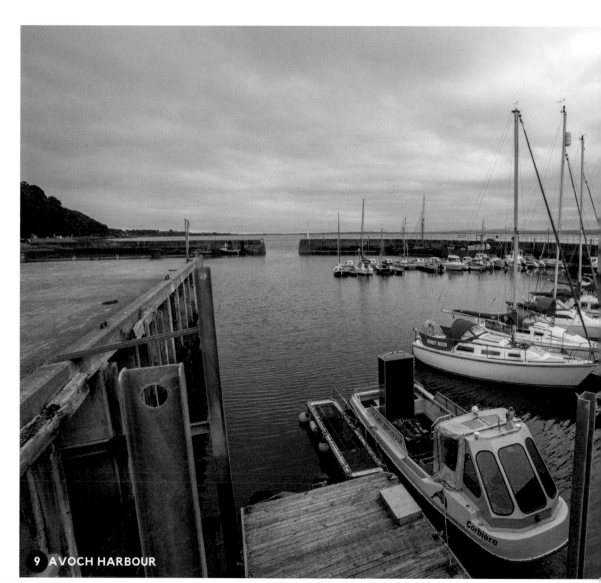

9 AVOCH HARBOUR

Where to Eat
in the Black Isle

Crofter's Bistro
A waterfront location with uninterrupted views over Rosemarkie Bay. With a large internal area for cosy dining and an outdoor patio area, this cafe offers a lovely and relaxed lineout.

-> 11 Marine Terrace, Rosemarkie, Fortrose IV10 8UL

Chanterelle Kinkell
A locally-owned, real-ale bar offering wholesome and warming meals with a relaxing atmosphere. It also has a beer garden and a variety of ales for you to enjoy with a view of the Moray Firth.

-> Easter Kinkell, Dingwall IV7 8HY.

Sutor Creek
A relaxed family restaurant offering Scottish seafood, seasonal menus and wood-fired pizzas. It has both lunch and dinner menus, as well as a beautiful view of the Cromarty Firth.

-> 21 Bank St, Cromarty IV11 8YE

North Kessock Hotel
This beautifully rennovated, family-run hotel offers luxurious, verandah al-fresco dining with views of the waterfront of the Beauly Forth.

-> Main St, North Kessock, Inverness IV1 3XN. Dog-friendly.

Shimla Tandoori Restaurant
On the southeastern border of the Black Isle, in the small town of Beauly, you can enjoy a taste of Scotland's Tandoori cuisine at the Shimla restaurant.

-> 3 High St, Beauly IV4 7BY

The Anderson
With a collection of over 260 single-malt whiskies, fresh real ales, a huge list of beers, this cosy traditional pub is an award-winning stop-off for your NC500 trip.

-> Union St, Fortrose IV10 8TD. Dog-friendly.

9 AVOCH HARBOUR

Where to Stay
in the Black Isle

Hotels in the Black Isle
- The Royal Hotel Cromarty
- Newhall Mains
- Allangrange Arms
- North kessock Hotel
- Muir Bank

Apartments in the Black Isle
- Longhouse Cottages
- The Mended Drum
- Culbokie Lodges
- Fishermans
- Kilcoy Chalets
- The Bothy

Campsites in the Black Isle

Fortrose Bay Caravan Park
Just off of the Chanonry Point peninsula, Fortrose Bay is a large campsite in the middle of the Black Isle. With 50 spacious sites and views over the Dornoch Firth, this is a very good site to visit.

-> Wester Greengates, Fortrose IV10 8RX

Rosemarkie Camping and Caravanning Club
On the other side of the Chanonry Point Peninsula from Fortrose, the Rosemarkie campsite sits on the shore with views to the north of the firth.

-> Bught Ln, Inverness IV3 5SR

Dingwall Camping and Caravanning Club
On the western shore of the Cromarty Firth, the Dingwall Campsite is a great base camp for those wishing to explore more of Easter Ross, west of the Black Isle.

-> Jubilee Park Rd, Dingwall IV15 9QZ

Road Trip Essentials
in the Black Isle

Food Shops
- Tesco Dingwall
- Costcutter
- Spar Rosemarkie
- Co-op Fortrose
- Morrisons Invergordon

Water Points
- Tore Service Station
- Morrisons Invergordon

Chemical Waste Disposal
- Black Isle Stud
- Beauly Holiday Park

7 CHANONRY POINT

8 FAIRY FALLS NATURE RESERVE

EASTER ROSS

Passing over the Cromarty Firth with the open ocean on your right, seals playing in the bay below and the towering silhoettes of the North Coast 500's first real mountains to your left, the size of the highlands begins to sink in as a stark contrast to the cute harbour towns of the Black Isle. Humbled by the size of the land of the giants that lies ahead, the winding road tells you only one thing; this trip is going to be a good one.

The area of Easter Ross is a rather unique part of Scotland due to the smooth blend of modern day life, historical townships and fishing villages, as well as the last remaining signs of a mysterious group of people who vanished from history centuries ago.

The western end of the county consists of the jagged peaks and gushing waterfalls of the central belt of the highlands, and the eastern shoreline is decorated with small harbour towns, golden beaches, and dramatic cliffs. The history of this region dates from the ancient civilsation of the lost Pictish people through the kings and queens of the middle ages, and onto the modern day distilleries of Glenmorangie, Dalmore, and Balblair.

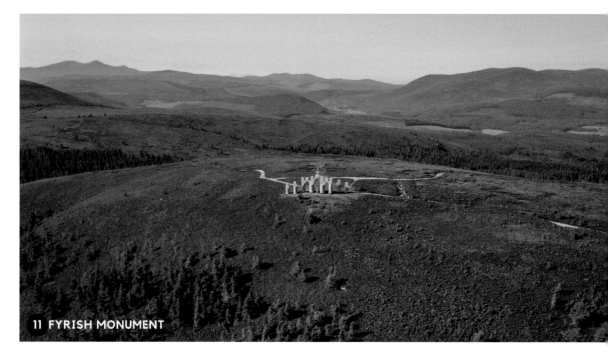

The region of Easter Ross is much wilder in comparison to the southern stops of Black Isle and Inverness. Spanning from the unforgiving mountains of the west across to the crashing shorelines of the unsheltered peninsula to the east, Easter Ross is the first true taste of wilderness that you will experience on your trip.

The region is the perfect place to dust off your hiking boots and get out amongst nature, filled with nature trails to explore, waterfalls to hike, and munros to bag. This was also one of the most notable areas on the NC500 for wildlife spotting when we toured the route, with the incredible number of seals that could easily be spotted on the shores of the Cromarty Firth as you drive along the A9.

11. Fyrish Monument

A fascinating tale of a shining light in one of the darkest times for the highlands of Scotland, the Fyrish Monument stands tall and proud as a reminder that kindness is always an option.

During the dark days of the Highland Clearances, Sir Hector Munro employed locals in need to construct this polylithic stone structure for no other reason than to keep them in work. It is said that he brought the stones one by one to the top of the hill so as to keep the locals employed for as long as possible.

Its design is based on the Port of Negapatam in Madras, India, a port that Sir Munro took for the British in 1781.

-> *Turn off the A9 onto B9176 and continue north before turning left after roughly 3km at the signpost to Boath (there is also a small, wooden signpost labelled "Fyrish Monument Car Park"). Follow this until you see the large car park on your left. The hike to the monument is reasonably strenuous and takes about 3 hours up and down.*

2. Black Muir Woods and the Touchstone Maze

 beautifully peaceful nature walk that is perfect for all of the family, this short circuit leads through
he tall woods of Strathpeffer with views west over the fields to Castle Leod and the mountains
eyond. There are two routes on offer; the Red Kite Trail and the Touchstone Maze Trail.

he Touchstone Maze itself consists of a spiral of stones that have been brought here from all across
he highlands and islands, showcasing the wide variety of geology that can be found in Scotland.
hey are laid in a pattern that reflects the locations where these rocks can be found across the
ountry.

 *Heading north on the A834, the entrace to Blackmuir woods is quite hidden, just beyond the grand white presence of the
effer Lodge. Turn right after this building and follow the narrow road past the signpost for Blackmuir woods until you reach
e car park at the end. Here you will find a map board detailing the route.*

3. Rogie Falls

 short walk ending with an impressive waterfall,
ogie Falls tumbles over three levels on the Black
Vater River. There is also a beautiful suspension
ridge that offers the best perspective of the falls
nd leads across the raging torrent below.

 *Car park is beside the A835, north of Contin. The path
 fairly flat and accessible, with a slight hill. Accessible for
lectric wheelchairs with off-road capabilities. Toilets in the car
ark area.*

12 BLACK MUIR WOODS

13 ROGIE FALLS

14 BEN WYVIS

14. Ben Wyvis

Ben Wyvis is a Scottish Munro located in Easter-Ross, north west of Dingwall. It sits at an elevation of 1046m, overlooking a number of surrounding mountains and farmland. Ben Wyvis is easily recognised as the a mountain that dominates the landscape in this region due to the long ridge at the summit.

The Scottish Gaelic name for Ben Wyvis is Beinn Uais, translated to "hill of terror". Whether this originates from an old tale about the hill or the near vertical ascent that you must overcome to reach its foreboding peak, we will leave that up to you to decide.

-> The car park sits on the side of the A835, 15 miles from Inverness. Follow the path along Allt a' Bhealaich Mhòir stream for around 2km, before following the path straight up the hill on the left and ascend to the top.

Note that the car park has a 2m height barrier and is unsuitable for vans.

5. Little Garve Bridge

 peaceful and easy going walking route along
e Black Water River, showcasing two beautiful
ridges that span the rushing water from the
aster Ross mountains.

his walk is particularily beautiful in Autumn
hen the leaves begin to turn a golden orange
d line the pathways.

Located on the A835. Car park to the south of Black Water
lls car park on the right of the A835.

16. Black Water Falls

A stunning set of waterfalls with a deep and
moody feel. The name of this river is fully justified
as the water runs as black and mysterious as the
dead of night.

The parking lot has a toilet and the path to the
falls is very accessible.

-> Located on the A835. Very clean toilet block open 24/7.
Peaceful spot with easy access to the waterfalls viewpoint.

16 BLACKWATER FALLS

17. Shandwick Stone

A remnant of the Pictish folk that once inhabited this area of Scotland before they mysteriously vanished in the early 10th-century.

The Shandwick Stone sits in a glass housing, guarded from the elements, overlooking Shandwick Bay.

Limited parking. Turn left when heading south on the B9175 towards Ankerville and follow the unnamed road until you see signposts directing to you to the stone to the right.

19. Mermaid of the North

Part of this region's Seaboard Sculpture Trail, the Mermaid sits on the shoreline at Balintore, isolated from the mainland at high tide. The bronze sculpture celebrates the lore of mermaids in this region of Scotland.

Parking at the Balintore Seaboard Centre, the mermaid sits on a rock about 200m to the south along the coast.

18. Portmahomack

A peaceful fishing village with beautiful golden beaches and crystal clear water. The perfect stop off if you are looking for a spot off-route and not overcrowded to grab a bite to eat.

Local amenities and shops for food and drinks.

-> Follow the B9165 as far north as it will go and you will reach Portmahomack. Plenty of small car parks, large enough for campervans and motorhomes.

20. Tarbat Ness Lighthouse

At the very northern tip of the Easter Ross peninsula is the guarding light of the Tarbat Ness Lighthouse. Built in 1830, this beacon has guided ships safely past the rocky cliffs of Easter Ross for centuries.

-> Large car park at the end of the single track road. Vehicles longer than 8m will have trouble turning.

9 MERMAID OF THE NORTH

17 SHANDWICK STONE

Where to Eat
in Easter Ross

Balintore Inn
Overlooking the sea, guests can enjoy a cold drink and hot meal either beside a log fire or in the beer garden with a stunning view.

-> East St, Balintore, Tain IV20 1UA

The Castle Hotel, Portmahomack
A friendly and traditional pub on the high street of Portmahomack, you can enjoy hearty pub meals and a refreshing drink here.

-> Pet friendly. Castle St, Portmahomack, Tain IV20 1YE. Dog friendly.

Platform 1864, Tain
Inside the town's former railway station, this quirky gastropub is Tain's newest established restaurant and bar. Offering everything from breakfast to evening meals.

-> Pet friendly. Station Rd, Tain IV19 1JA. Dog friendly.

The Seaboard Centre, Tain
A quiet cafe worth a visit in the small town of Balintore. This is the perfect spot to have lunch after visiting the Mermaid of the North and the Shandwick Stone.

-> East St, Balintore, Tain IV20 1UA

Meikle Ferry Station
Over 150 years old, this renovated ferry terminal now hosts a cafe/restaurant, as well as a 4 bedroom self-catering property.

-> Meikle Ferry Station, Tain, Highland, IV19 1JX

Harry Gow Bakery, Tain
A must-visit location on your NC500 trip, these bakeries are spread along the eastern coast of the route. Stop off and grab a classic pie or pasty before heading on your way.

-> 8 High St, Tain IV19 1AE

18 PORTMAHOMACK

Where to Stay
in Easter Ross

Hotels in the Easter Ross
Novar Arms Hotel
The Station Hotel
Tuckers Inn
Balintore Inn
Morangie Hotel Inn

Apartments in the Easter Ross
* Delny Highland Lodges
* Delny Glamping
* Kirkside Holiday Home
* Inver Bay Apartment

Campsites in the Easter Ross

Dornoch Caravan and Camping Park
North of the Easter Ross peninsula on the shore of the Dornoch Firth is the small and quaint town of Dornoch. A peaceful campsite and stop-off as you head northwards.
The Links, Dornoch IV25 3LX. Dog friendly.

Fortrose Bay Caravan park
Just off of the Chanonry Point peninsula, Fortrose Bay is a large campsite in the middle of the Black Isle. With 50 spacious sites and views over the Dornoch Firth this is a very good site to visit.
-> Wester Greengates, Fortrose IV10 8RX. Dog friendly.

Dingwall Camping and Caravanning Club
On the western shore of the Cromarty Forth, the Dingwall Campsite is a great base camp for those wishing to explore more of Easter Ross, west of the Black Isle.
-> Jubilee Park Rd, Dingwall IV15 9QZ. Dog friendly.

18 PORTMAHOMACK

18 PORTMAHOMACK

Road Trip Essentials
in Easter Ross

Food Shops
Asda Tain
Lidl
Tesco
Co-op Tain
Morrisons
Co-op Invergordon
Co-op Dalmore

Water Points
- Balintore Harbour
- Asda Garage Tain
- Morrisons Garage Invergordon

Chemical Waste Disposal
- Black Isle Stud
- Beauly Holiday Park
- Falls of Shin Visitor Centre

16 BLACKWATER FALLS

18 PORTMAHOMACK

22 EMBO BEACH

SOUTHEAST SUTHERLAND

The region of Sutherland dates back to a time that is so ancient it is often confined to works of fiction, alongside the lore of dragons, giants, and the fairies of the glen. Translating to "Southern Land", this bizarre description for one of Scotland's most northerly regions makes more sense when it is paired with the fact that the origin for this name dates back to the rule of Nordic forces, more often known as the Vikings.

This northern expanse of wildnerness and mountains is one of the most sparsely populated regions of mainland Great Britain, with less of a total population than a medium-sized southern town. Mainly located in the small harbour towns that you will pass through on the route, the population's main income is from the once-rich fishing industry that the open ocean provides.

Entering into this beautiful part of Scotland, with the endless moors and towering mountains, mirrored by the contrasting golden sands and dramatic cliffs along the coast, you can begin to understand why Sutherland is known as Europe's "last great wilderness".

22 EMBO BEACH

29 BIG BURN FALLS

Due to the incredible size of the region of Sutherland, as well as the fact that the North Coast 500 route leads you in and out of the area, we have decided to split the region of Sutherland into two areas: the Southeast and the Northwest. As with the rest of the NC500 route, the eastern region of Sutherland is slightly more developed than its western counterpart. This, of course, means that the southeast region of Sutherland is rich in history and culture, as well as draped in the stunning beauty of the Scottish landscape.

Starting at the Dornoch Firth, the Southeast region of Sutherland stretches along the eastern coast to the fishing town of Helmsdale. This area of the route consists of a mixture of jagged mountain peaks, still lochs, crashing waterfalls, and sleepy coastal towns, each with their own story to tell.

Contrasting with the wild and rugged northwestern coast of Sutherland, the southeastern end is dotted with civilisation both modern and ancient. Award-winning golf courses and fairytale castles sit side by side along this stretch of coastline, complimented with an untouched landscape and beautiful beaches that rival those anywhere else in the world.

1. Falls of Shin

Although not the most dramatic waterfall you will find in the region, these falls are one of Scotland's most significant due to the role they play in Scotland's ocean life. It is here at the Falls of Shin that you will be able to see the marvel of the leaping salmon, as they make their way inland to the still and safe refuge of Loch Shin to lay their eggs.

The best time of year to see the salmon is between May and September, however, as with any wildlife spotting, you will need to be patient in order to get a sighting.

Turn left from the A9 onto the A949 and follow it west through Bonar Bridge, continuing onto the A836 until you see signposts for the Falls of Shin. There is a large car park with motorhome facilities and a cafe/toilets.

2. Embo Beach

One perfect example of a golden Scottish beach, with a stunning background to match it. Embo Beach sits to the north of the town of Dornoch, beside the small town of Embo.

There are no facilities at this beach, however, the nearby town of Dornoch has public toilets.

Drive northwards out of Dornoch along Station Road until you see the sign to Embo turning to your right. Follow this and once you reach the holiday park make a left. Park where appropriate and walk to the seaside.

22 EMBO BEACH

23. Dornoch Town

One of the most historically significant towns on the route, Dornoch is a popular spot on the eastern coast of the route. It is easy to see why, with the beautiful architecture of the Dornoch Castle and Cathedral in the town centre to the golden stretches of sand that lines the coast.

The town of Dornoch is home to the Royal Dornoch Golf Course, ranking 13th in the world for best golf courses. It also has a very notable history as it is the location of the last ever witch execution in 1722.

>Turn right from the A9 and head east along the A949 until you reach the town centre of Dornoch. Parking is widely available across the town centre, particularly at Meadows Park. Toilets are available in the town centre.

24. Dornoch Beach

Stretching 4km from the car park at the northern end to the Dornoch Firth at the south, Dornoch Beach is an incredible expanse of golden sands and beautiful sea views. Due to the steady gradient of the beach, the range of tide at Dornoch Beach is incredible, with a low tide mark around 500m away from the high tide. If you want to swim you will need to visit at high tide.

>From Dornoch Town Centre, follow Golf Road to the end and you will find the car park.

25. Dornoch Cathedral

A former cathedral, this is actually now a Church of Scotland parish church. Despite no longer being the seat of a bishop, it still retains the cathedral name due to its history.

Built in the 13th-century, the beautiful arches and organs on the inside of the cathedral are a must-see attraction before you continue north.

->Park in the town centre and find the cathedral across from the Dornoch Castle hotel on Castle Street.

24 DORNOCH BEACH

26. Loch Fleet

Located by the small town of Golspie, the Loch Fleet Nature Reserve is a beautifully peaceful and secluded corner of Southeast Sutherland. This large estuary sits in the tidal basin north of Dornoch and is home to a magnificent selection of wildlife, from Arctic Terns and Oystercatchers, to Water Voles and Otters.

->*Continue north along the A9 until you reach Golspie and turn right along Ferry Road. Follow this for 3miles to Little Ferry and park here. There is a public toilet available in Golspie town centre.*

27 Highland Wildcat Trails

Described as the longest freeride descent in the UK, this mountain biking trail sits just outside the town of Golspie. The trail climbs the side of Ben Bhraggie to the 397m high summit, with incredible views of the distant Dornoch Firth. There are three available trails of various skill levels, ranging from 6.5km to 13.6km in length.

->*Driving north on the A9, take a left onto Fountain Road across from the Golspie Stone Shop. Follow this road past the monument and continue through the junction up the hill. You will find the car park on your right.*

28. Dunrobin Castle

Straight from the fairytales of your childhood, Dunrobin Castle's towering spires and beautiful gardens makes it one of Scotland's (if not the world's) most beautiful castles. Dating back 700 years, the castle itself is one of Britain's oldest continuously inhabited buildings, and it is the largest in the northern highlands of Scotland with a total of 189 rooms.

You can enjoy a self-guided tour of the castle's interior museum, as well as the falconry display that happens in the gardens for a fee. Visiting after closing time will allow access to the gardens for free.

->North of the town of Golspie on the A9, the entrance to the car park can easily be found on the right-hand side of the road. There is ample amounts of free parking here. It is also possible to catch a train from Inverness to the Dunrobin Castle station that sits outside the entrance to the castle, taking just over 2 hours.

28 DUNROBIN CASTLE

29. Big Burn Falls

A tranquil riverside walk that leads through the forest on the northern end of Golspie. The walk from the lower car park is an easy going route that takes about 30 minutes to reach the waterfall.

Along the route, the path passes through a deep gorge with multiple wooden bridges criss-crossing the river. A peaceful and beautiful route with an impressive waterfall to finish it off.

->Lower Car Park sits beside Golspie Inn. Upper Car Park can be found by taking next left on the A9 and following the road for 600m.

29 BIG BURN FALLS

29 BIG BURN FALLS

29 BIG BURN FALLS

30. Ben Bhraggie
An unmissable peak overlooking the Dornoch Firth bay, with the prominent silhoette of the 100 foot tall statue that marks the top of the hill. This statue is in honour of George Leveson-Gower, the first Duke of Sutherland.

A short 400m ascent from Golspie, the hike to the top takes roughly 2 hours in total and is quite a steep ascent with stunning views from the top.

->*The hike begins in Golspie town centre and heads to the north past the Highland Wildcat Trails. Parking is ample in the town centre and a toilet is available.*

31. Beinn Lunndaidh
The true peak of the ridge that marks the horizon overlooking the Dornoch Firth, Beinn Lunndaigh sits higher than its more famous summit, Ben Bhraggie.

The route starts at the same point as Ben Bhraggie, in the town centre of Golspie, and the route takes around 4 hours.

->*Similar to Ben Bhraggie, there is ample parking in Golspie town centre. The route takes you past the Highland Wildcat Trails and continues up the hill.*

33 LOCH BRORA

2. Brora Beach

With panoramic views over the horizon of the North Sea, Brora Beach in an excellent place for wildlife spotting, with frequent sightings of dolphins, minke whales, seals, and porpoises. This combined with its beautiful soft sands, nearby amenities, and picturesque golf course, Brora Beach is the perfect place to stretch your legs, explore the nearby town, and if you are lucky, soak up some much anticipated Scottish summer sun.

>Driving north along the A9, turn right at the Coop in Brora town centre. Follow this road until you see signs for the campsite and the beach car park. Follow these signs to reach the medium sized car park. Public toilets are available in the town centre, behind the Coop.

3. Loch Brora

A mostly under-appreciated location on the North Coast 500, Loch Brora sits inland from the quaint town of Brora, hidden from the busy northern road trip and the bustle of every day life. The still waters of this loch and the silhouettes of the guarding mountain ranges all around makes it a beautiful place to explore.

There is a small beach not far from the car park , which combined with the gentle incline into the water of the loch makes it the perfect spot to enjoy some watersports on Loch Brora. Stand Up Paddleboard rentals are available in the town of Brora with Sutherland Adventure Company.

>Cross River Brora driving north on the A9 and immediately turn left onto the smaller country road. Follow this road to the west until you reach the loch and there is a small car park on the left with a short walk to the water.

Where to Eat
in Southeast Sutherland

Cocoa Mountain, Dornoch
One of two cafes on the NC500 route, the hot chocolates on offer here are sheer decadence. Rich and creamy hot chocolates with hand-crafted chocolate "chasers" to go on the side. A must-try stop on this route.

-> Castle St, Dornoch IV25 3SN. Dog friendly.

Clynelish Distillery
Sitting outside Brora, this distillery is known as one of the Four Corners of Johnnie Walker as it supplies a vital component to this famous blended whisky brand. Tours and tasting sessions are available here.

-> Clynelish KW9 6LR

Sid's Spice, Brora
Voted second best Indian restaurant in Scotland, this is a definite food stop for any curry lover. Offering both dine in and takeaway options, you can enjoy your curry wherever you fancy.

-> Sid's Spice takeaway, Station Square, Brora KW9 6QJ.

Golspie Inn, Golspie
Located in the quaint town of Golspie, this beautiful inn offers hot meals and refreshing drinks that are perfect for after your hikes in the local area.

-> Old Bank Rd, Golspie KW10 6RS. Dog friendly.

Harry Gow Bakery, Brora
A bucket-list bakery on the NC500, this chain of cafes are spread across the southeast of the route, meaning this is your last chance to try it if you are heading north.

-> Rosslyn St, Brora KW9 6NY

Cocoa Skye, Brora
Offering the most luxurious brunch in the region (if not the entire route), this Brora cafe has a huge range of delicious waffles and ice creams, as well as other breakfast and lunch items.

-> London House, Station Square, Brora KW9 6QJ.

33 LOCH BRORA

Where to Stay
in Southeast Sutherland

Hotels in SE Sutherland
Golspie Inn
Dornoch Castle Hotel
Links House Dornoch
Royal Marine Hotel Brora
Sutherland Inn Brora

Apartments in SE Sutherland
- NC500 Glamping Pods Brora
- Anvil House Golspie
- No.2 The Links
- The Apartment at Allt-Sagart Golspie
- The Tall Pines Yurt and Studio

Campsites in SE Sutherland

Dornoch Caravan and Camping Park
North of the Easter Ross Peninsula on the shore of the Dornoch Firth is the small and quaint town of Dornoch. A peaceful campsite and stop-off as you head northwards.
The Links, Dornoch IV25 3LX. Dog friendly.

Pondside Camping & Accommodation
Nearby the banks of Loch Shin, this inland campsite is the perfect base camp for exploring both the southeast and the northwest of Sutherland.
-> 4 Tirryside, Lairg IV27 4DL. Dog friendly.

Brora Caravan and Motorhome Club Campsite
Just 200m from Brora Beach, this campsite offers incredible views over the North Sea, perfect for wildlife spotting and relaxing escapes to the north coast.
-> Dalchalm, Brora KW9 6LP. Dog friendly.

26 LOCH FLEET

Road Trip Essentials
ı Southeast Sutherland

ood Shops
Lidl Tain
Asda Tain
Tesco Tain
Coop Golspie
Coop Brora
SPAR Lairg

Water Points
- Falls of Shin
- Helmsdale Harbour
- Camping@Golspie
- Lairg Filling Station

Chemical Waste Disposal
- Falls of Shin
- Camping@Golspie

28 DUNROBIN CASTLE

CAITHNESS

Venturing into the most northerly region of the British Mainland, it is evident that the land around you is steeped in history. The sea cliffs to your right are dotted with the remains of ancient castles, the boglands further inland sit as desolate and uninhabitable as they have for thousands of years, and the very name of the land you travel through derives from the words of a lost and mysterious race of people.

Caithness, named after the Pictish "Cat" people and the Nordic word "Ness" meaning "headland", is the 700-sq mile section of land on the most northeasterly point of Scotland's mainland. The landscape of this northern area of Britain is quite shocking compared to the rest of the Scottish highlands, mainly due to how flat in profile the land is, as well as the distinct lack of natural forests.

This level profile and lack of any form of natural woodland is due to the incredible size of bogland that makes up a lot of the area of Caithness is known as the Flow Country, and is noted as one of the largest boglands in Europe. With the modern day problems our planet faces, this enormous "carbon sink" plays a crucial part in the capture and storage of carbon dioxide from the Earth's atmosphere.

42 DUNCANSBY HEAD STACKS

34 DUNBEATH BAY

The namely desolate lands of Caithness have provided a safe haven for wildlife and the ancient history of Scotland, protecting both from destruction by modern society. As you travel north and turn westwards through Caithness, be sure to note and appreciate the distinct lack of any signs of modern-day society that can be found in between the quaint and welcoming towns that you pass through on your road trip.

This section of the North Coast 500 has the largest number of castle structures, both lying in ruin and maintained in their beauty. As the road winds along the coastline of the north of Scotland, it also introduces some of the most beautiful beaches that can be found in the country, a lot of which are an easy walk from your vehicle.

As you continue on your journey through Scotland's most remote wildernesses, it is here in Caithness that you will experience any real form of township, with the large dwellings of Wick and Thurso offering the last real chance to enjoy civilisation. This will be your last chance to visit a supermarket or nightlife until you return to the northern capital of Inverness, so be sure to spend some time in these towns before you continue on your journey into the unknown and wilderness that lie to the west.

34. Dunbeath Bay

A quaint and beautiful fishing village that sits removed from the daily rush of the busy A9 above. The harbour of Dunbeath offers a fantastic view of the local shingle beach and the impressive silhouette of Dunbeath Castle in the distance, which sits perched on the edge of the cliff, high above the crashing sea waves below.

->Turn right off the A9 after the bridge over Dunbeath Bay. Take the first left and follow the narrow road to the harbour. Public toilets and parking can be found here.

35. Castle of Old Wick

Perched in solitude upon a narrow promontory between two towering cliffs, the Castle of Old Wick is an impressive sight to behold. This once four-storey stronghold now lies in ruin, with the majority of its stone structure falling victim to nature. It is believed to date back to the 14th-century, although these details remain shrouded in mystery.

->North on the A99, turn right onto March Road, before the retail outlet, and continue along to the end of the road. There is a small car park nearby the castle.

36. Whaligoe Steps

Hidden on the eastern edge of northern Scotland is one of the most remarkable man-made constructions in the United Kingdom. The winding, limestone staircase of the Whaligoe Steps dates back hundreds of years to the days when this tiny harbour was one of the most important in the region. Numbering 330 in total, the steps lead down to the remains of Whaligoe harbour, which once hosted up to 14 boats of the local fishermen. Landing their daily catch here in the harbour, the fishermen and their families would then need to carry it up the winding staircase, all the way to the top.

->Signposts direct you to turn right from the A99 to the Whaligoe Steps car park. Alternative parking can be found by turning left instead, leading to Loch Watenan. The steps are great in number and will require a level of fitness to climb. Don't descend unless you are confident you can get back up. Cafe at the top with great views.

36 WHALIGOE STEPS

37 CASTLE SINCLAIR AND GIRNIGOE

7. Castle Sinclair and Girnigoe

The largest castle ruins on the NC500 are the cliffside wonders of Castle Sinclair and Castle Girnigoe. The 15th century Castle Girnigoe and 17th century Castle Sinclair are believed to be one of the earliest seats of Clan Sinclair. Perched on the side of the cliff, the castle was constructed between 1476 and 1606, with adaptions made to it spanning some 100 years. Occupation of this castle came to an end in 1680 when a siege to Castle Sinclair and Girnigoe saw it damaged so badly, it was never inhabited again.

This castle site is free entry, although there is a donation box on the gate. Reconstruction of the ruins aims to make Castle Sinclair the first castle on the North Coast 500 to be wheelchair accessible.

->*Take the eastern route out of Wick, heading towards the sea, following signs for Noss. Park at the Noss Head Car Park and walk across the nearby field, following signposts, for about 600m. Entry on donation basis.*

8. Noss Head Lighthouse

Derived from the Nordic word "Snos", meaning nose, Noss Head Lighthouse sits on the very edge of the Wick headland. Perched on one of the NC500's most easterly points, this is a top spot for enjoying the sunrise over this 19th-century lighthouse.

->*Follow above directions to Castle Sinclair and Girnigoe and walk from the car park to the lighthouse.*

39. Sinclairs Bay

This bay stretches from Noss Head all the way north to the small town of Keiss. This stunning bay is lined with golden sandy beaches, Reiss Sands to the south and Keiss Beach to the north. It is a very popular spot for surfing and wildlife enthusiasts with frequent seal spottings.

->*The best vantage points can be found at Noss Head (see left), or either Reiss or Keiss beaches.*

37 CASTLE SINCLAIR AND GIRNIGOE

40 OLD KEISS CASTLE

40. Old Keiss Castle

Perched perilously close to the edge of a cliff, the open ocean raging below on stormy nights, this castle is like something from a movie. Built in the early 16th century, it has since been replaced by the new Keiss Castle, which sits further inland. Due to the decaying state of the castle it is not possible to visit it. Instead enjoy the view from a distance.

->The castle sits on private land and can only be reached by walking from Keiss town centre. Park here and make your way to the coast, before turning north towards the castle. Path is fairly rough. Toilets in Keiss.

41. John O'Groats Signpost

One of the most popular sights on the NC500 and a main feature on a lot of UK traveller's bucket lists, the famous signpost can be found beside the John O'Groats visitor centre. It is free to visit the signpost, however, be aware that you will need to queue for a picture due to its incredible popularity.

->Heading north on the A99, follow signs for John O'Groats Harbour. Parking is available here and is Pay and Display. Toilets available for a fee. Cafes and tourist shops also available here.

2. Duncansby Head Lighthouse and Stacks

Perched off the northeast corner of the British mainland lies the natural wonder of the Duncansby Stacks, as well as the lighthouse that guards these perilous shores. These 60m sea stacks tower high above the ferocious and unpredictable water of the North Sea. It is a land carved by time and stands as a monument to the destructive power of nature in this part of the world.

Built in 1924, this lighthouse remained home to a keeper for over 70 years until 1997, when it was fully automated and no longer required a resident. The lighthouse tower remains here to this day, still functional, protecting boats from the crags and cliffs of this notorious span of water.

->Driving north on the A99, before you reach the turn for John O'Groats Harbour, turn right at the fuel station and follow this road until you reach the car park at the lighthouse. There is a large car park here with no facilities.

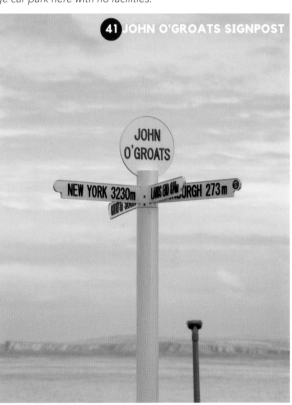

41 JOHN O'GROATS SIGNPOST

43. Bay of Sannick

A hidden gem in Caithness, the Bay of Sannick is another perfect example of Scotland's beautiful golden beaches, guarded by rugged cliffs and breathtaking sea views. This beach sits just to the west of Duncansby Lighthouse and is often overlooked by visitors racing onto the next stop on the North Coast 500.

->Driving towards Duncansby Head, there is a small parking spot on the left with room for 3 cars. Head through the small gate and walk until you see the beach.

42 DUNCANSBY HEAD STACKS

120

46 DUNNET BEACH

44. Castle and Gardens of Mey
Built in the 16th century, the Castle and Gardens of Mey sit on the northern coast of Caithness, beautiful and picturesque against the endless horizon to the north. Maintained by the Castle of Mey Trust, it is possible to explore the internal rooms as well as the gardens by paid entry and experience the grandour and history for yourself.

->Heading west on the A836, follow signposts for the castle by turning right fom the main road. The car park lies at the end of this road. Toilets and cafe are available here.

46. Dunnet Beach
South of the lighthouse peninsula, this great, sweeping arch of golden sand is known as Dunnet Beach. Sheltered from the savage waves of the open ocean, this beach is a fantastic spot for surfers, dog-walkers, and any other beach-lovers on the northern coast.

->Heading west on the A836, the car park for the beach sits beside the entrance to Dunnet Bay Campsite. Toilets are available here, as well as a small shop.

45. Dunnet Head Lighthouse
The most northerly point of the British mainland, Dunnet Head is home to the beautiful structure that is Dunnet Head Lighthouse. Built in 1831, this lighthouse stares out into the great beyond of the North Sea, warning ships against the dangers of the jagged cliffs below.

->The lighthouse can be reached by the B855 in Dunnet town then by following this road, continue onto the car park that lie at the end of the narrow, winding road.

45 DUNNET HEAD LIGHTHOUSE

7. Sandside Bay Beach

A secluded and quiet beach on the northern coast with a darker history than the golden sands may let on.

In 1977, a small explosion at the nearby Dounreay Nuclear Power Station was heard early in the morning. Since that day, small pieces of radiated material have been discovered on this beach and the surrounding area. Whilst admiring the beauty of Sandside Bay, make sure not to take anything home with you due to this danger.

->Heading west on the A835, turn right after Reay Golf Course and follow the road. A toilet block is available.

48. Puffin Cove

A beautiful spot that sits hidden beneath the radar and out of sight of the main road, the small beach known as Puffin Cove is one of the most unique spots in Caithness.

Named after the large colonies of puffins that use this protected bay to rest and shelter from the savage North Sea, this is one of the best spots to see these cute and often elusive birds.

->Car park sits beside Caithness sign post nearby Melvich. Path down is very rough and can be dangerous.

48 PUFFIN BAY

Where to Eat
in Caithness

Whaligoe Steps Cafe
A haven at the top of the 300 steps of Whaligoe Haven, this cafe is a wonderful place to stop off for a coffee and homemade cake with a view over the cliffs below.

->The Square, Ulbster, Lybster KW2 6AA. Dog friendly.

No1 Bistro, Wick
Located at Mackays Hotel in the busy town of Wick, this restaurant prides itself in the use of locally sourced ingredients for the spectacular range of Scottish cuisine it has to offer.

->Ebenezer Pl, Wick KW1 5BX.

Storehouse, John O'Groats
Part of the John O'Groats accommodation, the Storehouse is a modern cafe serving a range of light-bites and meals. It is also a licensed bar, so if you are staying in the area, stop by here for a drink.

->The Storehouse, John O' Groats KW1 4YR

Castletown Chip Shop, Thurso
A highly recommended chip shop serving up freshly caught fish not far from the beautiful stretch of sand that is Dunnet Bay. No better place to get a takeaway to enjoy fish and chips on the beach.

->MacKay St, Castletown, Thurso KW14 8UQ

Y-Not Bar and Grill, Thurso
With live music, a range of cocktails and spirits, cold beers, and delicious food on offer, this bar/restaurant is a great place to relax and unwind in Thurso's town centre.

->Meadow Ln, Thurso KW14 8ER. Dog friendly.

Harbour Chip Shop, Wick
In the town centre of Wick, this small chip shop is another highly recommended takeaway on the NC500 route. Enjoy a chip shop takeaway with harbour views before you continue on your trip.

-> Harbour Quay, Wick KW1 5EN.

34 DUNBEATH BAY

Where to Stay
in Caithness

Hotels in Caithness
- The Portland Hotel
- Ulbster Arms Hotel
- Mackays Hotel
- Seaview Hotel
- Station Hotel

Apartments in Caithness
- North Coast Escapes
- Harbour View Apartment Wick
- North Star Glamping

Campsites in Caithness

Wick Caravan and Camping Site
A family run campsite overlooking Wick River, this spot offers a secluded, picturesque and tranquil setting to rest up on your road trip. There are electric hookups, hard-standing pitches and a well-kept toilet and shower block.
> Riverside Dr, Wick KW1 5SP. Dog friendly.

John O'Groats Campsite
Perched at the very end of the British mainland, this campsite sits right beside the famous signpost in John O'Groats. Adjacent to all of the bars and cafes of the tourist centre. This large campsite also has electric hookups and soft and hard pitches.
-> County Road, John o' Groats KW1 4YR. Dog friendly.

Inver Caravan Park
Adjacent to the A9 and easy to find, this small campsite outside Dunbeath has nearby shops and is just a short walk to the tranquil harbour of Dunbeath. Offering hard-standing pitches and electrical hookups, as well as grass pitches.
->Houstry, Road, Dunbeath KW6 6EH. Dog friendly.

41 JOHN O'GROATS SIGNPOST

Road Trip Essentials
in Caithness

Food Shops
- Costcutter Lybster
- Lidl Wick
- Coop Wick
- Tesco Wick
- Lidl Thurso
- Tesco Thurso
- Coop Thurso

Water Points
- Lybster Harbour
- Keiss Aire
- Bridgend Filling Station Thurso
- Small Croft (KW3 6BA)

Chemical Waste Disposal
- Small Croft (KW3 6BA)

35 CASTLE OF OLD WICK

37 CASTLE SINCLAIR AND GIRNIGOE

NORTHWEST SUTHERLAND

he most north-westerly regions of the British Isles introduce a new meaning to
ne word "remote". As the road winds its way throught the towering rocky outcrops
nd spots of formidable moorland, still lochs lie dotted amongst the dramatically
ndulating landscape, and the natural wildlife that seems all but forgotten
lsewhere in the world roams wild and free.

Vinding through the formidable terrain of the Durness Peninsula, the desolate wasteland
f Cape Wrath, and along the winding and narrow roads of the western coastline, it is
ifficult to not experience an overwhelming admiration for the beauty that lies before you.
is here, deep in the highlands of Scotland, far from city life and the normality of modern
ociety, that most visitors come to the great realisation of their true and forever-welcoming
ome; the bonnie land of Alba.

82 CLASHNESSIE BAY

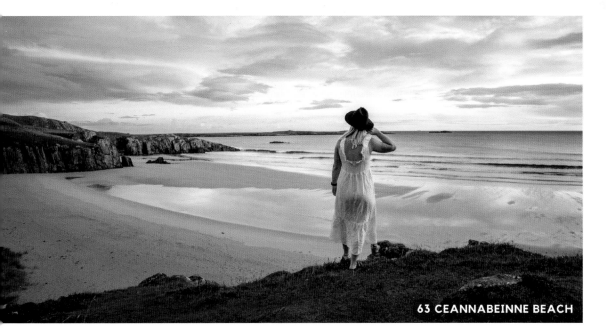

63 CEANNABEINNE BEACH

is here in the wonderful northwest region of Sutherland where the sunrises nd sunsets turn the sky to a hue that has never been witnessed anywhere else n earth. Crystal-clear waters of tropical torquoise wash upon soft white sands, uarded by inaccessible mountains, entirely untouched by mankind. Silent othies sit far from civilisation, offering shelter to weary travellers desperate for spite from the relentless and unforgiving winds that have shaped this dramatic ndscape over millions of years.

ntirely contrasted with the inhabited southeastern region of the county of Sutherland, e northwest is more comparable to a different world than just a different side to the untry. The dramatic and weathered mountains that line the western side of Scotland t high above the deep lochs that line their endless ridges. The road suddenly drops to ngle track as you enter the narrow and winding passes between the ancient giants that dormant on either side.

e scenery starts to make you question every definition of beauty that you thought you ew. As you drive along the open and vulnerable pass of the Tongue Causeway, your flection keeps pace on the still water beneath and the mountains in the distance barely em to move at all, giving significance to their unfathomable size and solitude.

e next couple of hundred miles of the road trip through the NW of Sutherland consist ainly of hidden, inaccessible beaches, inviting lochs of tranquil beauty, and a dominating rizon lined with an uncountable number of mountain peaks.

50 STRATHY BEACH

49. Melvich Beach

This crescent shaped beach of golden sands and crashing waves is guarded by the sand dunes that run along its southern edge. Make your way through the tall grass and stop to admire the beautiful wild flowers that decorate the dunes in Springtime. This beach is especially breathtaking at low tide, as the sea retreats to show the golden expanse of soft sand.

->Driving west along the A836, the car park for Melvich Bay sits down a rough, single track road on the right. It is a medium sized car park with no facilities.

50. Strathy Beach

One of the most picturesque beaches on the northern coast, this beach is guarded by towering cliffs to the east and the River Strathy to the west. Quite inaccessible, with a steep, long climb down to the beach itself, the Strathy Beach car park offers a breathtaking vantage point above the wide bay and distant cliffs. This isolated beach is well worth the journey if you wish to make the climb down.

->Turn right off the A836 heading west at the North Coast Parish Church. Follow this road to the car park at the end. Toilet facilities can be found here.

51. Strathy Point Lighthouse

Built in 1958, this lighthouse sits isolated at the very northern end of the Starthy Peninsula. Hidden by the rolling and rocky hills of this desolate stretch of land, the lighthouse has now been converted to accommodate travellers for both long-term and short-term stays.

->Take the exit from the A836 west of the Strathy Inn and follow the narrow, winding road to the end. Park here and walk the rest of the way to the lighthouse.

52. Farr Beach

A sheltered and shallow sloping beach, this bay sits to the northeast of Bettyhill. The slow gradient of the bay means there is a dramatic difference between high tide and low tide on this beach.

At low tide, the golden and beautiful sands stretch for hundreds of metres out to sea, giving plenty of room to explore and marvel at the incredible views of the bay.

->There is parking just to the west of the Bettyhill Tourist Centre. Park at the side of the A836 and walk down the lane to the bridge and cross to reach the beach.

52 FARR BEACH

52 FARR BEACH

54 COLDBACKIE BEACH

53. Skerray Bay

A quiet and secluded harbour on the north coast, this bay is a favourite of many visitors with its stunning views across the water to the isolated Neave Island, and peaceful atmosphere of the harbourside. Recommended for a tranquil lunch spot and relaxing sea swim, Skerray Bay is well worth a visit on your road trip.

->The route to Skerray Bay leads you around a loop from the A836, through Bourgie to the northern coast, and returns to the A836 further west via Modary. There are no facilities at this harbour.

54. Coldbackie Beach

Protected by a near inaccessible hike and guarded by the sand dunes that lie along its southern edge, Coldbackie Beach is one of the most beautiful and isolated beaches on the North Coast 500 route. As you drive along the cliffside road towards Tongue, a glimpse of the blue water and golden sands comes into view, tempting even the most hurried traveller to pull over and admire the stunning views of the bay below.

->Heading west on the A836, the beach lies far below the road on the right. There is a small parking area at the side of the road with an information board.

55. Tongue

Showing the old Norse influence on the region, the name of Tongue descends from this ancient language referring to the shape of the land resembling a spit or a tongue. The history of this town dates back to the 15th century when the distinct outline of the castle on the hill was in full use.

This was also the scene of a battle between Jacobite and Royal Navy vessels in 1746, where the Navy came out victorious thanks to the help of the locals. This proved a costly loss to the Jacobites later at the deciding battle of Culloden.

Following the A838 you pass through Tongue. There is a public toilet, as well as a good cafe in the hotel.

56. Castle Varich

The unmistakable silhouette of this ancient castle sits on a prominent hill above the town of Tongue. The ancient seat of Clan Mackay, this site is thought to be over 1000 years old.

The current remains were built on top of the remains of an old Nordic fort, providing a natural vantage point over the incoming bay, and it is even believed that there are caves under the castle that were once inhabited by Clan Mackay.

->Park beside the public toilets in Tongue and follow the footpath that begins at the signpost beside the RBS building. From here there is a reasonably strenuous walk along the path to the castle.

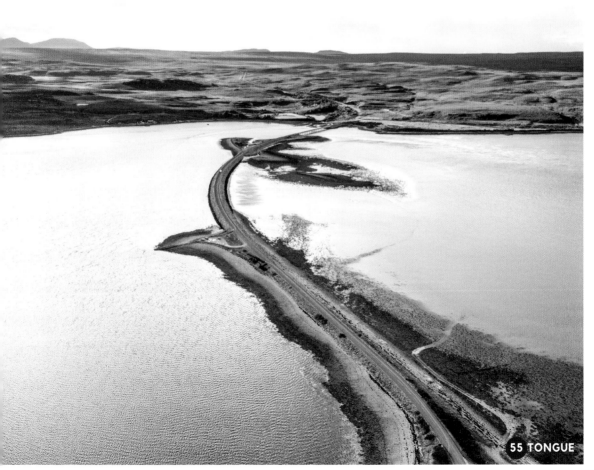

55 TONGUE

57. Loch Craggie Viewpoint

Sitting high above the serene and tranquil Loch Craggie, with incredible views through to Ben Loyal to the south, this viewpoint is marked by a small car park at the side of the road. There are some very interesting information boards, all about Sutherland and the surrounding area. This is a great spot to stop and admire the views of the glen below, and doubles as a great overnight spot for responsible campers.

->*Continue on the A836 by turning south before Tongue and follow the road until you find the car park.*

58. Ben Loyal

The distinct and impressive outline of this corbe dominates the skyline of Tongue, its unmissable presence leading to it being nicknamed the "Queen of the Scottish Mountains". The long ridge of this mountain pairs with three others an provides spectacular views of the surrounding landscape. It is a tricky climb, with an easy beginning quickly turning into a boggy and unmarked track up the steep ascent.

->*Park beside the Castle Varich path (see previous page) and continue south. Refer to an OS map for guidance.*

59. Talmine Bay

Over the narrow causeway that leads across the Kyle of Tongue away from the town of Tongue lies the small string of settlements that make up the crofting township of Talmine. Lying far from the main road that leads the NC500 west, this lesser known and mostly undiscovered bay is one of the reasons why exploring Scotland in greater detail is so rewarding.

Following the narrow and winding road north from the A838 towards Talmine, the beautiful view of the still and shallow water of the Kyle to the right is difficult to describe. Golden sand beneath the water turns the coastline around Talmine a bright torquoise, contrasted by the dark and mysterious islands that lie distant to the north. A breathtaking part of this incredible Scottish coastal route.

->*Take the first right after the Kyle of Tongue Causeway and follow the narrow road towards Talmine. There is a small car park beside Talmine Bay with no facilities.*

60 ACHNANCLACH BOTHY

57 LOCH CRAGGIE VIEWPOINT

0. Achnanclach Bothy

Jestled beneath the steep slopes of Cnoc
a Moine, across the narrow strip of land that
eperates Loch Craggie and Loch Loyal, this
mall shephard's hut sits hidden from civilisation.
popular stopover for hikers bagging munros
nd corbetts in the region, this bothy contains
wo fireplaces, cooking equipment, two sleeping
latforms, and even a room with two spring
eds. A very luxurious exception to the bluepirint
f highland bothies.

>Park near the circular wall beside Loch Loyal and cross the
ridge to the stretch of land between the lochs. This path
continues for 1.5km to the bothy.

61. Ben Hope

The most northerly munro in Scotland, this
is a bucketlist mountain for any hill walking
enthusiast. This isolated giant offers a relatively
quick munro experience, with the route to the
top taking just 9km up and down. This, of course,
means a very steep ascent of 935m to the top
of this spectacular monolith. The walk is straight
forward, with a path and marker cairns marking
the way. Stunning views of the surrounding
countryside at the top.

->Before Loch Hope, turn south and follow the narrow road
until you see the sign "Way Up Ben Hope". Small car park with
no facilities.

59 TALMINE BAY

62 BALNAKEIL BEACH

2. Balnakeil Beach

..n isolated and peaceful beach north of Durness, his beach lies wide and long on the neck of araid Head. This beautiful beach is a popular pot for dog walkers and other locals, as well as ravellers in the area due to its beautiful views out o sea to the north. Visit the Cocoa Mountain cafe or the best hot chocolate in the area.

Continue straight following signs to Balnakeil. Continue ong this road till you reach the car park.

4. Sango Sands Beach

One of the northern coasts most famous eaches, Sango Sands sits beside the town f Durness and is overlooked by arguably the host scenic campsite in the world.

he viewpoint is accessed through this campsite nd gives a great vantage point over the blue ater and golden sands below.

Park beside public toilets in Durness and head towards he coast. Through the gate leading to the campsite, the ewpoint sits above the beach.

63. Ceannabeinne Beach

This beach sits under the mountain Beinn Ceannabeinne who juts proudly out of the landscape, 383 metres high. This is a hugely popular spot on the NC500, marked by the foreboding wires of the Golden Eagle Zipline that runs between the cliffs above the beach. A highly recommended activity on this route.

There is free parking overlooking the beach, however, you can expect this to always to be very busy with surfers, walkers, and other outdoor enthusiasts.

Further along the road, there is also the fascinating Ceannabeinne Village Trail, which tells the story of how the infamous Highland Clearances affected this isolated region of Scotland.

->The car park sits by the side of the A838 before the township of Sangobeg. No facilities here apart from a rubbish bin.

65. Kyle of Durness

The body of water separating the towns of Durness and Balnakeil from the desolate wilderness of Cape Wrath, the Kyle of Durness continues the theme of stunning views over crystal clear water with a backdrop of towering mountains. There is a small car park with an information board on the region just as you leave Durness, however the drive alongside the water is picturesque enough if you don't have time to stop.

->Follow the A838 through Durness and you will see the car park on your right. No facilities are here.

66. Faraid Head

Stretching out to the north from the town of Durness, this headland sits mostly desolate, aside from the MOD training facility that can be found at its northern end. Lined by golden sands and inhabited by roaming cattle, this peninsula is only accessible by foot, with no road leading out to it as it consists mainly of sand and grass.

->Park at Balnakeil Beach (see previous page) and walk along the beach to access the headland. There is not much of a path along the peninsula.

66 FARAID HEAD

67. Kearvaig Bothy

This is Scotland's most northerly and arguably most isolated bothy. Accessible by either a grueling, day-long hike through the Cape Wrath wilderness, or by catching the Cape Wrath Ferry and walking along the road from here, this bothy is a reward for the most daring adventurer. The bothy itself sits above the golden Kearvaig Beach and is an incredibly tranquil place to spend the night. Definitely a Scotland bucketlist item.

Accesible either by the Cape Wrath ferry or a hike across the Cape Wrath Peninsula. OS Map required.

68. Strathcailleach Bothy

Situated just to the north of the isolated Sandwood Bay, this bothy was home to one James McRory-Smith for over 40 years. It was taken over by the MBA in 1999 and now acts as a refuge to those brave enough to take on the wilderness of the Cape Wrath Peninsula. Occasionally used for military training, access is strictly prohibited when red flags are flying.

->Best accessed from Sandwood Bay, the trek out to this bothy is only recommended to experienced navigators with the help of an OS map and compass.

69. Sandwood Bay Beach

This mile-long stretch of sand is the location of possibly the most bizarre experiences that the NC500 has to behold. Involving a 4 mile hike along a rough dirt road, filtering down to a narrow walking track, this beach sits completely isolated far out on the Cape Wrath Peninsula. It is incredibly popular for such a remote part of the country and the experience of bumping into another wanderer so far out in the wilderness and swapping tales of what sights and wildlife you have seen is definitely one to remember.

->Park up at the Blairmore Car Park and begin the walk north to Sandwood Bay. The route is roughly 4 miles in total, stretching along a dirt track road for around 3 miles, before changing to a single lane walking track for the final stretch. It is a fairly easy-going walk until you reach the steep descent down sand dunes to the beach itself. Not wheelchair accessible due to rough terrain.

70. Oldshoremore Beach

Famous for being one of Scotland's most beautiful beaches, the crystal clear water of Oldshoremore makes for a remarkable sight on the northern coast. Facing westwards from the southern end of Cape Wrath, sunsets from this stretch of golden sand are simply spectacular. The dramatic tide at this beach means there is a great difference between high and low tides, with barely any sand on show at the highest of tides.

->*Leaving the main road to Kinlochbervie, heading northwards, Oldshoremore has a big car park with toilets and rubbish bins.*

71. Ben Stack

A prominent conical mountain marking the skyline of the North West Sutherland Scenic Area, this graham (a hill over 2000ft) dominates the horizon to the south of Laxford Bridge. The view from the top of Ben Stack delivers stunning views down the southeastern glen over the body of water known as Allt Ceann Locha. The view across Loch Stack towards the sister corbetts Foinaven and Arkle is also spectacular on a clear day.

->*South of Loch Stack, a small car park sits at the side of the A838. From here follow the OS map route towards Ben Stack. Compass required.*

72. Kinlochbervie

The most northerly port on the northwest of the British mainland, this tiny, scattered harbour town was mainly developed as a fishing hub, where ships from both east and west would land their catches. With a population of just over 400 people, this is a beautifully quiet town off the main route of the North Coast 500 has an enchantingly slow pace of life and a scenic backdrop to match.

For any campervan travellers, this is also the spot of a fantastic harbourside aire, offering drinking water and waste disposal for a small donation. One of the most scenic harbours on the route.

->*Leave the A838 at Rhiconich and turn northwards onto the B801, following this until you reach the harbour town at the end of the road. Toilets, a small shop, and chemical waste disposal are available here.*

70 OLDSHOREMORE BEACH

73. Wailing Widow Falls

A spectacular, 50ft waterfall that can be viewed from either above or below, these falls are accessible by a short (yet rather tricky) walk across boggy terrain.

The view from the top sits over a perilous drop with an overhang on the edge of the cliff, so be extremely careful.

Not advised for small children or dogs off a lead.

>*The top car park sits above of the winding pass beside Loch na Gainmhich, and the lower car park at the bottom. From either, follow the path towards the loch to reach the waterfalls.*

73 WAILING WIDOW FALLS

73 WAILING WIDOW FALLS

74. Castle Ardvreck and the White House

One of the most dramatic castle ruins you will find in Scotland, perched out on an island accessible only by a narrow band of shingle beach, the ruins of Castle Ardvreck are a stunning sight on this route. Situated right beside the main road, this castle has a fascinating story to tell, one dating back to the 16th century, and referring to the violent battles in this region between warring clans.

The castle was originally built by the Macleods of Assynt in 1590, however, it was attacked and captured by Clan Mackenzie in 1672, when they took control of Assynt lands. The castle stands today in ruin and is said to be the site of multiple ghost sightings of the weeping daughter of the Macleod Chief, who took her own life after being fooled into marrying the Devil.

->*The castle sits at the side of the A837, unmissable on its island on Loch Assynt. There are two car parks at the side of the road, neither offering any facilities or waste disposal. Viewpoint is wheelchair accessible, however, the ruins are not.*

75. Scourie Bay

On the western coast of the small town of Scourie, this sheltered bay faces west out to the open ocean, offering a spectacular location for a sunset by the sea.

This is a popular spot for SUP and sea kayaking due to the protection of the Scourie harbour and the still water on its coastal side. The campsite that sits above it is a beautiful location to spend the night on your trip.

->*The town of Scourie sits on the A894, with parking for the beach situated just to the west of the campsite.*

75 SCOURIE BAY

74 CASTLE ARDVRECK

76 KYLESKU BRIDGE

76. Kylesku Bridge

One of Scotland's most technically innovative bridges, set with a stunning backdrop of the mountains of Assynt, the Kylesku Bridge is one of the NC500's most iconic sights. Built in 1982, the bridge has now been awarded a classification as a Category A structure by Historic Environment Scotland, recognising it as "visually striking and technically innovative".

>There are two car parks on the A894, before and after the bridge with waste disposal. Viewpoint wheelchair accessible.

77. Arkle

Sister mountain to Foinaven that sits to the south, Arkle is another corbett that makes up the Assynt Skyline. The main feature of this mountain is its spectacular curving ridge of quartzite rock, formed 530 million years ago and thrusting up from the ground over time. It is a longer walk of around 11miles and can prove technically difficult towards the end with the exposed ridge.

->Leaving from the Ben Stack car park (see previous pages), head east across the spit of land between the lochs and follow the path for Arkle. OS Map required.

78. Handa Island

Sitting isolated off the coast of the Scottish highlands is one of the most significant breeding grounds for seabirds in the region. Recognised as an island of national importance, Handa Island is a Scottish Wildlife Trust reserve and is home to tens of thousands of sea birds that flock to the island every spring.

Vast numbers of Guillemots, Razorbills and Great Skuas spend their summers here, breeding and feeding in the rich waters that surround the island. It is possible to visit by boat and spend the day wandering around the wild and wonderful island, learning about the importance of the habitation for these beautiful birds.

>The Handa Ferry leaves from Tarbet harbour, which is situated just north of Scourie. Follow signs for the turnoff to the harbour and follow the road to the sea. Toilets are available by the harbour.

80 ACHMELVICH BEACH

79. Quinaig
The dominating silhoette that fills the skyline when you cross the Kylesku Bridge, the Quinaig is a hugely popular mountain in this region despite it falling short of Munro status.

The hike consists of a total of three corbett summits and is a length of roughly 9 miles. Mostly made up of good paths with minimal scrambling, however, it can prove steep in parts. Definitely one for experienced mountaineers.

->Car park sits south of the Wailing Widows Falls, at the side of the A894. Large and unmissable car park.

80. Achmelvich Beach
Hidden along a narrow winding road on the north west coast of Scotland is one of the most popular beaches on the North Coast 500, Achmelvich Bay. Surrounded by sand dunes and cliff faces, the white sandy beaches are met with the clearest of blue waters.

Being on the west coast of Scotland, Achmelvich Bay is a great place to watch the sunset from the beach over the sea.

->Follow the A837 south to Loch Assynt and onto Lochinver, then turn onto the B869 and follow signs. This beach is accessed by foot from a medium-sized car park. Toilets available in car park.

1. Old Man of Stoer and Lighthouse

A spectacular sea stack perched off Sutherland's most westerly peninsula. To the west of Clashnessie, the Stoer Lighthouse and sea stack can be found along the most westerly coastline of the area.

The walk to the stack begins at the lighthouse and journeys north for 2 miles across a sometimes pathless bogland. Not recommended on windy days due to danger posed by cliff drops.

->Driving north on the B869, follow signs for the lighthouse and continue to the car park at the west end. Set off north on foot and take care along the cliffs.

82. Clashnessie Bay

Clashnessie Bay is a small and beautiful bay with a rocky inlet and plenty of pristine white sand meeting the tranquil turquoise water. Clashnessie Beach has a mild micro-climate due to the closeness of the Atlantic Ocean Gulf Stream.

This peaceful spot is popular with the nearby locals, with stunning views of the bay from the overlooking cliffs and benches that can be found there.

->Continuing north along the B869 from Achmelvich. The road is narrow and winding, not recommended for caravans.

83 Clachtoll Beach

Overlooked by the nearby campsite, the continuing theme of the Sutherland beaches is reflected here with white sands and crystal clear waters.

This is a hugely popular wildlife spotting location, with frequent sightings of basking sharks, dolphins, and other marine life and birds off shore and along the cliffs.

->Beach accessible by driving through the campsite to the public car park. From here, there is a short boardwalk to the beach. Wheelchair accessible to a certain point where the boardwalk ends. Toilets available.

83 CLACHTOLL BEACH

82 CLASHNESSIE BAY

84. Clashnessie Falls

A deceptively long and difficult trek with an incredibly rewarding view to finish it off, the trek to Clashnessie Falls takes around 30mins and sonsists of frequent scrambles and boggy stretches. The 15m waterfall that sits at the end of the hike may not be the tallest on the route, however, the volume of water and width of the falls makes an impressive sight nonetheless.

->Heading south from Clashnessie, follow signposts from the beach car park across the boggy and rough path to the falls.

86. Lochinver

The small fishing port of Lochinver is the closest thing to civilisation that you will find between Scourie and Ullapool.

Full of delicious restaurants, shops for restocking, and a stunning view out to sea to the west, this quiet harbour town is a great place to stop off on your road trip to relax and refuel as you head south.

->Located at the western end of the A837. Toilets, shops, and chemical waste disposal available here.

85. Hermit's Castle

One of the most unique and slightly bizarre sights you will find on this road trip, Hermit's Castle is a concrete structure perched on the edge of the small cliffs that dot the coastline around Achmelvich. Camouflaged against the grey and green backdrop, this monument was built in 1950. The question of "why" it was installed, however, still hangs shrouded in mystery.

->Walk through the Shore Caravan Site and through the fence on the northern side. Continue west to the coast, over the rocks and you will see the castle.

85 HERMIT'S CASTLE

86 LOCHINVER

87. Falls of Kirkaig

A beautifully peaceful walk through the woodland to the south of Lochinver to the impressive 18m waterfalls known as the Falls of Kirkaig. The hike is a round trip of roughly 8km, taking 3 hours in total, and the path to the waterfall is fairly straight-forward, well-marked and only slightly rocky in places.

Great care is needed during the final descent to the falls as the path is steep and slippery with a fatal drop to the side.

->Large car park sits to the east of Inverkirkaig. Walk from here east through the gate following the river.

88. Suilven

One of Scotland's most famous and iconic mountains, Suilven is more comparible to the mountains of fiction and fairytale than those in Scotland. The silhouette of the near vertical graham is unmistakable upon the horizon as you head south through Assynt.

The hike to the razorback ridge of the Suilven is very steep, gaining almost 500m of elevation in just 1km. A high level of stamina is required, however, the path is easy to follow.

->East from Lochinver, park in the area at the roadside at the end of the public road and continue east on foot.

88 SUILVEN

89. Allt nan Uamh (The Bone Caves)

Just over a century ago, this seemingly empty and unimportant limestone glen was the site of a fascinating, bizarre and slightly haunting discovery; the multiple caves that lined the glen were filled with the numerous bones of ancient predators that once roamed the wilderness of Northern Scotland.

The skelatol remains of arctic foxes, wolves, lynx, brown bears, and even polar bears were all uncovered during an excavation, leading these caves to become known as the Bone Caves. The walk to the caves is quite flat until the final ascent, and leads through a beautifully tranquil glen surrounded by towering cliffs and roaming deer.

->East of the peak of the Canisp mountain, the car park sits on the left as you head south on the A837. Medium sized car par that gets busy quick. Walk to the caves is on an obvious path and takes roughly 1hr return. Not wheelchair accessible.

89 ALLT NAN UAMH (THE BONE CAVES)

90. Ardmair Beach

A rocky, shingle beach just outside of the town of Ullapool with spectacular views of Isle Martin and the open ocean to the west.

The dramatic tide at this beach will mean a vast difference in high and low tide, with the water lapping on the grass bank at the highest of tidal marks.

->*Located north of Ullapool on the main A835 southern route. Beside the Ardmair caravan park.*

92. Stac Pollaidh

A very popular peak to summit in the area with its low altitude (2000ft), easy access, and incredible views from the top, Stac Pollaidh features quite a unique summit with numerous limestone pinnacles along its ridge.

The hike requires a reasonable level of fitness and extreme care at the top, due to its steep drops and technical scrambles.

->*A circular route beginning on the northern coast of Loch Lurgainn. Car park sits on the lochside. From the car park, cross the road and head through the gate in the fence onto the footpath.*

91. Rhue Lighthouse

Marking the northern border of the loch to the ships making their way into the loch and onto Ullapool, the 37m outline of the Rhue Lighthouse makes for a beautiful sight against the picturesque backdrop of the distant shapes of the Summer Isles.

->*Car park sits at the end of the lighthouse road, heading west from the A835. From here, head off on foot towards the lighthouse across a grassy path.*

90 ARDMAIR BEACH

93 KNOCKAN CRAG

93. Knockan Crag National Nature Reserve

Another seemingly unimportant region of beautiful Scottish wilderness, it is here at the visitor centre where a discovery of the Moine Thrust was made. This discovery revolutionised the thinking of the scientific community during the 19th century.

Known as the Moine Thrust, the hills in this region were formed as the two continents collided and pushed up the lower layers of rock, creating the bizarre phenomenon of older rock sitting atop much younger rock. Here you can touch the very history that formed this dramatic and mountainous land with your bare hands.

->*Visitor centre lies above the A835 as you drive south.*

94. Elphin Tearooms

This cute and cosy cafe is a popular stop on the A835, serving warming teas and coffees, handmade cakes and light bites, as well as a range of locally made crafts and artwork.

This is the perfect place to stop off for a refreshing drink and a mooch for local souvenirs for your trip.

->*Turning west from the A837 onto the A835 at the Ledmore Junction, the tearooms can be found in the picturesque and quiet township of Elphin. Open Sat-Thurs until 31st Oct, and Sundays only through winter.*

Where to Eat
in Northwest Sutherland

Cocoa Mountain, Durness
Home of decadance, this chocolate cafe serves up some of the richest drinks on the northern coast. Partnered with the sister cafe in Dornoch, this is a must-visit spot in NW Sutherland for any sweet tooth.
->Balnakeil, Durness, Craft IV27 4PT. Dog friendly.

The Chippy, Ullapool
The most popular chip shop on the western coast of the NC500, this gourmet fish bar serves fresh fish on a daily basis, as well as unique and delicious vegetarian options.
->Quay St, Ullapool IV26 2UE. Dog friendly.

The Strathy Inn
Just a short walk from the beautiful Strathy Beach on the northern coast, Strathy Inn has a cosy restaurant and bar with incredible views over the open moorland to the south. Relax by the fire and enjoy a warm pub dinner.
->Strathy, Thurso KW14 7RY

The Ceilidh Place, Ullapool
The cosy and quirky cafe/bar/restaurant in Ullapool's town centre is guaranteed to satisfy any and all visitors to this northern capital. Serving up delicious meals, cold drinks, and sometimes live music.
->West Ln, Ullapool IV26 2UT. Dog friendly.

The Elphin Tearooms
Serving up a range of handmade cakes, scones, and light bites such as soups and sandwiches, these tearooms are a popular stop-off on the road from Scourie to Ullapool.
->The Elphin Tearooms, Elphin, Lairg IV27 4HH. Dog friendly.

Peet's, Lochinver
Sitting right in the centre of the Lochinver Harbour, this restaurant serves up fresh seafood in a traditionally Scottish style. It also has a varied "from the land" menu, as well as numerous vegetarian options available.
->Culag Rd, Lochinver, Lairg IV27 4LE

Where to Stay
in Northwest Sutherland

Hotels in the NW Sutherland
- Kylesku Hotel
- Bettyhill Hotel
- Inver Lodge Hotel
- Eddrachilles Hotel
- The Tongue Hotel
- Smoo Lodge

Apartments in NW Sutherland
- 4 Wheelhouse Apartment
- Rustic Cabins
- NC500 Pods, Achmelvich
- Achmelvich View, Self-catering

Campsites in the NW Sutherland

Clachtoll Campsite
Overlooking the stunning Clachtoll Beach, this campsite offers a mixture of serviced and unserviced, soft and hard standing pitches. Not far from the town of Lochinver.

->134, Clachtoll, Lochinver, IV27 4JD. Dog friendly.

Sango Sands Oasis
Famous for being one of the country's most scenic campsites, Sango Sands Oasis sits high up on the cliffside above the beautiful Sango Sands beach.

->Sangomore, Durness IV27 4PZ. Dog friendly.

Scourie Caravan Park
Sitting above the scenic and tranquil Scourie Bay, which sits sheltered by the harbour that stretches across the bay. This peaceful spot is a popular launching point for kayakers.

->Scourie, Lairg IV27 4TE. Dog friendly.

Road Trip Essentials
n Northwest Sutherland

Food Shops
Durness Shop
SPAR Kinlochbervie
Drumbeg Stores
SPAR Lochinver
Tesco Ullapool

Water Points
- Blairmore Public Toilets
- Kinlochbervie Harbour
- Scourie Filling Station
- Lochinver Leisure Centre

Chemical Waste Disposal
- Kinlochbervie Harbour
- Lochinver Leisure Centre

80 ACHMELVICH BEACH

WESTER ROSS

A landscape made from some of the oldest rocks in the world, the mountains and glens of Wester Ross have existed long before the first footfalls of mankind and will continue to stand long after the last. This part of Scotland once sat all but covered by giant glaciers, carving out the deep glens and forming the modern sea-lochs that it is characterised by today.

Its beginning is marked by the small hub of Ullapool, one of the only respites from the wild on the western coast, and it is the final stretch of the route that leads around Scotland's northern coast. Continuing the theme of dramatic horizons, towering peaks, crashing waterfalls, and remote and untouched beaches, the region of Wester Ross is mainly inhabited by small fishing villages and remote country escapes.

The dramatic landscape of Wester Ross has widely prevented the development of any civilisation and giving safehaven to wildlife across the region, with a huge number of seabirds, marine mammals, and wild deer sighted frequently across the land.

The narrow, winding roads continue south through the landscape of Wester Ross making driving along this stretch of the NC500 an interesting task, with the constant distractions of stunning lochs and distant mountains. This section of the route has some of the most notable stretches of road of the entire road trip, from the famous and controversial rise of the Bealach na Ba pass, to the incredible, winding road that leads through Glen Docherty.

It is common for visitors to the North Coast 500 to begin to rush their journey when they reach this section of the trip, as traveller fatigue begins to set in and the road stretches out in front. However, this is the part of the road trip that proves to be the most rewarding to any visitor bold enough to slow down and appreciate the slow pace of life of the highlands.

Enjoy the frequent view points along the route, visit the numerous golden beaches, and attempt to bag some of the iconic munro mountains as you meander through the region of Wester Ross, then stop off at the sleepy harbour towns for a relaxing coffee and cake. Whatever you do, however, don't forget to make the most of your time in this beautiful part of the world as this is the home stretch of your epic road trip.

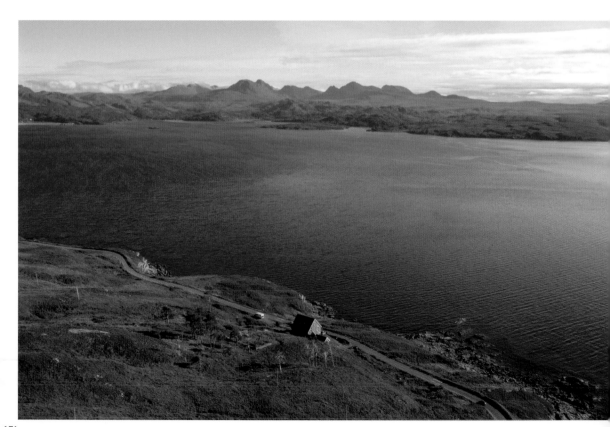

95. Ullapool

The largest habitation on Scotland's northwestern coast, the harbour town of Ullapool is home to around 1,500 people, and acts as the central hub for exports to the remote islands of the Outer Hebrides. Protected by the surrounding ridges of the mountains that tower over Loch Broom, Ullapool offers possibly one of the most picturesque town views in the highlands.

Enjoy your time in this buzzing and welcoming highland town by visiting one of the many bars and restaurants that line the seafront street, offering stunning views down the loch towards the southern end of Loch Broom.

->The main road of the A835 passes directly through the town centre of Ullapool before turning south along the edge of Loch Broom. Plenty of parking available in the town centre, along the harbour street or by the Tesco. Toilets available inside the shop or at the public toilets for a fee.

96. Corrieshalloch Gorge

The crashing water of the 46-metre tall Falls of Measach thunder down the incredibly impressive ravine known as the Corrieshalloch Gorge.

Sitting about 20km to the south of Ullapool, this National Trust site features a suspension bridge spanning the deep gorge, as well as a viewing platform that looks back towards the bridge and the impressive waterfall beneath.

->Turning south from the A835 onto the A832, the car park for Corrieshalloch sits on the right. Free parking for NTS members. Wheelchair accessible, however, there is a slope.

96 CORRIESHALLOCH GORGE

98 FIREMORE BEACH

97. Mellon Udrigle
Mellon Udrigle Beach is another spectacular beach that sits off the beaten track of the main NC500 tourist route. It is well worth the drive along to this secluded settlement as the white sandy beach has beautiful views of the mountains. There is a small car park with a short wooden boardwalk along the beach. There are no facilities nearby this beach, however, there is a campsite if you are looking for somewhere to stay the night in the area.

->*Leaving the A832 north at Laide, this beach sits on the narrow road, signposted Mellon Udrigle.*

98. Firemore Beach
A beautiful stretch of sand located near Poolewe, Firemore Beach is often missed out on many people's NC500 itinerary due to it being a bit of a detour from the route. However, this beach is brilliant for watersports and even swimming as the water is the warmest you will find on the west coast of Scotland due to the Gulf Stream running close by. If you are patient enough, dolphins, whales and seals have been spotted from the shoreline.

->*Turning north after Poolewe, leave the A832 past the Poolewe Hotel, continuing along this road to Firemore.*

97 MELLON UDRIGLE

99 GRUINARD BEACH

99. Gruinard Beach

The stunning stretch of red sand along the southern end of Gruinard Bay is a beautiful place to explore, popular with dog-walkers and other beach-goers exploring the route. The water of the large bay sits extraordinarily clear at high tide, creating a beautiful orange and teal effect when looking back towards the bay from the elevated viewpoint further south.

->Further along the A832, following the coast of Little Loch Broom, the car park for Gruinard Beach sits on the left across from the lower beach. No facilities.

100. An Teallach

Widely noted as one of Britain's most dramatic peaks, the towering, jagged ridge of An Tealach is an iconic sight in the region of Wester Ross. It is a difficult climb to make beginning with a boggy trek and ending in a perilous scramble along the knife-edge ridge. This walk is not to be taken lightly by any adventurer, however, it is well worth it if you know what you are doing.

->Walk begins at the large layby beside the Dundonnel Hotel. OS Map required.

101. Inverewe Gardens

Meeting point of the Gulf Stream and the highlands of Scotland, the unique microclimate of Loch Ewe and Inverewe provides the perfect habitat for the fascinating range of rare species that decorate the Inverewe Gardens.

A formerly barren part of the highlands, this part of Wester Ross began its conversion into the colourful array of exotic and native plants and trees in 1854. The surrounding area of Poolewe is even host to "Scotland's Big 5" animals: Red Squirrels, Red Deer, Otters, Seals, and even the elusive Golden Eagle, so keep your eyes peeled!

->The gardens sit on the northern hill from Poolewe, overlooking the northern section of the bay of Loch Ewe. There are shops, campsites, and toilets available in the town itself.

102. Gairloch Beach

Gairloch Beach is a secluded bay surrounded by mountains and moorland located on the southern outskirts of Gairloch. This beach is popular with families and is enjoyed by many at sunset due to the westerly position of the beach.

Down on the sandy beach there are incredible views across to the nearby islands. There is free Parking for the beach beside the golf course.

->Continue south from Gairloch along the A832, the car park can be found across from the old church. Toilets available on walk to beach. CDP at nearby harbour.

103. Slioch

Eight kilometres from the town centre of Kinlochewe sits the rocky fortress of the Slioch mountain. A hugely popular mountain for photographers and walkers alike, this is one of the area's most iconic peaks, unmissable against the dramatic horizon. With a total ascent of 1200m across 19km, this route is one for the more experienced mountaineers.

->Leaves from the Incheril Lodge Car Park at Kinlochewe.

102 GAIRLOCH BEACH

101 INVEREWE GARDENS

104. Big Sand Beach

This large, unspoiled stretch of golden sand sits just outside the small village of Gairloch. Sheltered by the small, uninhabited island of Longa Island, Big Sand Beach offers a welcome break from the relentless wind of the North Atlantic.

Make your way through the grass dunes and enjoy the stunning view of the distant Herbides, especially during one of Scotland's famous golden sunsets.

->Heading west from Gairloch, leave the A832 and drive along the B8021 until you reach the campsite.

105. Victoria Falls

Named after a visit by Queen Victoria in 1877, Scotland's answer to South Africa's towering giant sits not far from the beautiful Loch Maree. Easily accessible by wheelchair, a flat, dirt path leads out to the viewing platform, which offers a great view of the cascading water into the lower gorge.

->Located on the southern side of the A832 that runs along Loch Maree. A small car park with no facilities.

105 VICTORIA FALLS

104 BIG SAND BEACH

06. Glen Docherty

An incredibly picturesque view that symbolises all that the highlands of Scotland have to offer. From the Glen Docherty viewpoint, the winding road of the A832 leads down through the tranquil glen towards the still waters of Loch Maree.

A breathtaking location for a picnic, or a simple break from Scotland's winding roads.

->Continue south from Loch Maree, through Kinlochewe and pull into the car park at the top of the hill. Rubbish facilities available.

106 GLEN DOCHERTY

107. Beinn Eighe

West of the highland town of Kinlochewe, the towering trinity of Torridon peaks guard the lower banks of Loch Maree. The most prominent peak of this ridge is Beinn Eighe, which stands 1010m tall, and is a hugely popular munro, which features a well-walked path up its steep slopes to its rocky and rough ridgeline. A good walk for experienced hikers.

->Continuing south from Kinlochewe along the A896, the car park for Beinn Eighe lies on the right. A large, tarmac car park with no facilities.

108. Craig Bothy

Dotted far out on the stretch of desolate and forgotten land north of Loch Torridon sits the secluded and incredibly peaceful hut known as Craig Bothy.

Situated on the banks of the Craig River, the hut is only accessible by foot, however, it may be one of the most luxurious bothies in the MBA's collection. Not only does it have two large downstairs rooms, it also features three upstairs rooms, and even a toilet out the back.

->Leaving from Diabeg to the south, the walk to the bothy is 3 miles long and is on a fairly easy-going path.

111 APPLECROSS

09. Shieldaig

ounded in the 1800s, this small harbourside
llage was developed with the aim to train
eamen for the upcoming war against Napolean.
emote and hidden from the shoreline, this
llage was the perfect place for such a goal,
ven providing trees for the warships from the
nall forestry island that sits across the water
om the town.

oday it sits as a small and peaceful fishing
llage with stunning views through Loch
orridon to the open ocean.

*The village centre sits just off the main A896 road. Follow
gnposts to the village seafront. Toilets available.*

110. Beinn Damh

Dominating the skyline to the south of Upper
Loch Torridon, this corbett features a dramatic
eastern ridge with steep drops of Torridonian
sandstone.

Despite its seemingly impregnable peak, the
walk to the top is actually much more relaxed
than some of its neighbouring mountains.
Following an easily visible path almost to the top,
the walk is tough but enjoyable for experienced
hill walkers.

*->Begins in the car park beside the Torridon Inn on the
southern edge of Upper Loch Torridon. OS Map required.*

111. Applecross

Hidden from the rest of the country, far out to the west on the almost inaccessible Applecross Peninsula, this small town offers a lone refuge from the wilderness of the Wester Ross landscape. There are only two ways to access the quaint and quiet town of Applecross, either by the winding coastal road around the northern edge of the peninsula, or by the mountainous route known as the Bealach na Ba, one of the highest roads in Britain.

In the town itself, you will find the reassuring sight of the Applecross Inn, a warm and welcoming escape from the unpredictable conditions of the highlands of Scotland. Live music, warming meals, and a friendly, highland atmosphere, this inn draws visitors from all across the country, so make sure to book a table if you wish to dine in.

->Follow signposts either around the northern coast or through the Bealach na Ba. Campsite and public toilets available.

112. Bealach na Ba

The Pass of the Cattle. This winding and perilous road was once the only route to and from Applecross and its sister settlements on the coast of the Applecross Peninsula.

It is one of the steepest roads in the UK, climbing to 626m above sea level, and it is not suitable for large vehicles or learner driviers due to the hairpin bends and steep drops. It is also often impassable in winter.

->Following the A896 south, the turn for this road is beside Tornapress, crossing the River Kishorn.

111 APPLECROSS

13. Eilean Donan Castle

he iconic sight of these beautiful castle ruins sits guarded by the still waters of the intersection etween Loch Duich, Loch Alsh, and Loch Long. Aside from the dramatic and breathtaking scenery at sits as a backdrop to this castle, the history of the region itself is reason enough to visit.

his castle began its life as a way of guarding the entrance of Loch Duich against the increasing umber of Viking raids. Eventually the castle was reduced to ruin during the Jacobite rebellion, hen government forces took the castle and destroyed it to prevent it from being used as a ortification in the future.

lthough it is not strictly on the North Coast 500 route, the castle is one of the most photographed ortifications in Scotland, being featured in countless Hollywood movies, such as James Bond as the 16 headquarters, and is a must-visit spot in the region.

Heading south of Strathcarron, the return leg to Inverness to finish off the North Coast 500 route takes you along the A87 ad. The castle sits just offshore of this road, with a large car park and visitor centre. The best view can be found at the Dornie ommunity Hall. Public toilets available here.

Where to Eat
in Wester Ross

The Chippy, Ullapool
The most popular chip shop on the western coast of the NC500, this gourmet fish bar serves fresh fish on a daily basis, as well as unique and delicious vegetarian options.
->*Quay St, Ullapool IV26 2UE. Dog friendly.*

The Ceilidh Place, Ullapool
The cosy and quirky cafe/bar/restaurant in Ullapool's town centre is guaranteed to satisfy any and all visitors to this northern capital. Serving up delicious meals, cold drinks, and sometimes live music.
->*West Ln, Ullapool IV26 2UT. Dog friendly.*

The Applecross Inn
Decorated with wooden beams and an array of whiskies along the bar, this warm and cosy pub offers the perfect highland welcome as you journey through the wilderness of Wester Ross.
->*Shore St, Applecross, Strathcarron IV54 8LR. Dog friendly.*

The Gairloch Hotel
A bespoke and luxurious hotel overlooking Gairloch Bay and the distant silhoettes of Longa Island and the Isle of Skye, the restaurant offers an exquisite range of local and European cuisines.
->*Gairloch IV21 2BL. Dog friendly.*

The Strathcarron Hotel
This family run hotel and pub/restaurant serves up warm and delicious meals with a friendly and welcoming atmosphere. It also offers a stay the night scheme for motorhomes to sleep in the car park with use of toilets.
->*Station Road, A890, Strathcarron IV54 8YR*

Inverewe Gardens
This National Trust site offers a range of hot and cold meals to be enjoyed with stunning views from the floor to ceiling windows that line the cafe walls
->*Poolewe, Achnasheen IV22 2LG. Dog friendly.*

111 APPLECROSS

Where to Stay
in Wester Ross

Hotels in the Wester Ross
- Poolewe Hotel
- Torridon Resort
- Gairloch Highland Lodge
- Tigh an Eilean Hotel
- Ledgowan Lodge
- Gairloch Hotel

Apartments in Wester Ross
- Bothan Dubh Cabins
- Sound of Durnamuck
- Edindoune, Strathcarron
- Zenka, Port Henderson

Campsites in the Wester Ross

Applecross Campsite
This large campsite offers spaces for serviced and unserviced vehicles, as well as pitches for tents. There are also onsite caravans and huts that are available for rental. It is an easy walk away from the Applecross waterfront.
->Applecross IV54 8ND. Dog friendly.

Broomfield Holiday Park
Overlooking the beautiful Loch Broom, this campsite sits in the heart of Ullapool. Famous for its stunning scenery and close proximity to the vibrant town of Ullapool, this is a hugely popular place to stay.
->West Ln, Ullapool IV26 2UT. Dog friendly.

Sands Caravan and Camping
Further away from the busy A832 main road, the Sands Campsite overlooks the stunning stretch of beach known as Big Sands. This is a peaceful campsite with beautiful views and friendly staff.
->Gairloch IV21 2DL. Dog friendly.

Road Trip Essentials
in Wester Ross

Food Shops
- Torridon Stores and Cafe
- Shieldaig Stores
- SPAR Lochcarron

Water Points
- Gairloch Harbour
- Torridon Public Toilets
- Shieldaig Public Toilets

Chemical Waste Disposal
- Gairloch Harbour

PLANNING YOUR ROUTE

One of the best parts of the North Coast 500 route is the incredible depth and breadth of attractions that can be found throughout the landscape. From castles to waterfalls, ancient history to modern day highland culture, there are so many fascinating sights and breathtaking places to visit in the highlands of Scotland that one trip is simply not enough.

In order to make the most of your time in Scotland, we highly recommend spending longer in each of the locations that we have listed above, diving deeper into the local lifestyle and spending time soaking up the beauty that is around you. It is, therefore, recommended that you break the route down into different sections and visit each location over the next few years. This way you can experience the joy of slowly falling in love with a country, its sights, smells, sounds, and most of all, its people.

Of course, it is not always possible to visit a country as many times as we would wish, and so to help you plan the perfect road trip on the NC500 here are some itineraries for the route, showcasing the best sights that you simply cannot miss.

28 DUNROBIN CASTLE

How to Spend 5 Days on the NC500

With only 5 days to drive the entire 516-mile route of the NC500, the main focus is going to be on the picturesque western coast of the route. Start the day off early in Inverness, heading directly north through the Black Isle, Easter Ross, and into the wilderness of southeast Sutherland.

Day One - Start off the day with a hot chocolate to remember at *Cocoa Mountain in Dornoch*, enjoyed with a relaxing walk along the beautiful stretch of golden sand that is *Dornoch Beach*. From here, head north to the fairytale fortress of *Dunrobin Castle* and enjoy either a guided tour of the inside of the castle, or a simple stroll through the gardens below.

After exploring this castle, it is time to head into the northern region of Caithness, stopping off for a quick climb down the stunning *Whaligoe Steps* to the isolated harbour at the bottom. Continue north onto the ancient ruins of *Castle Sinclair and Girnigoe* to enjoy a wander through one of Scotland's most impressive castle ruins.

To finish off the first day on the route, what better place is there than the most northeasterly point of the British mainland, *John O'Groats*. Here is the best place to spend the night, either on the campsite, or in one of the local hotels, enjoying the stunning view of the islands and open ocean to the north as the sun paints the sky a golden colour to the west.

Day Two - Heading over the hills to the east of the *Duncansby Lighthouse*, kick off the second day with an incredible view of the *Duncansby Stacks* (best enjoyed at sunrise). From here it is time to turn west along the northern coast, through the northern town of *Thurso* and out towards *Strathy Point Lighthouse*. Pull into the *Strathy Beach* parking lot for a quick glance at the stunning beach that lies below, sheltered by the surrounding cliffs, before you continue on to the lighthouse itself.

The next stop lies far to the west, back into the northwestern reach of the region of Sutherland. As you wind your way along the narrow road towards the town of *Tongue*, keep your eyes peeled to the coastline below on your right for the secluded and secretive *Coldbackie Beach*. Take your time as you head down the hill onto the beach and enjoy the isolation that the high sand dunes provide from the road that winds around the cliff edge high above.

Cross over the *Kyle of Tongue Causeway* and continue west soaking up the stunning views of the mountains and lochs that are dotted along the route until you reach the town of *Durness*. Check into the campsite overlooking *Sango Sands beach*, or into a hotel in the local village and relax after another busy day on the route.

Day Three - Turning south, it is time to move onto the most impressive section of the NC500 route. The first stop on the western coast lies far to the south at the small harbour of *Tarbet*, where you can catch a rib across to the beautiful refuge of *Handa Island*. Exploring this island will take a couple of hours and the last boat to reach the island leaves just after lunch, so make sure to leave early.

Crossing the iconic *Kylesku Bridge* and admiring the stunning backdrop of the region of *Assynt*, the journey continues southwards to the central hub of *Ullapool*. Stop off at the *Knockan Crag Nature Reserve* to learn about the fascinating geological phenomenon that this part of the world has on display, before driving to the town of *Ullapool* to spend the night.

95 ULLAPOOL

Day Four - Begin the day nice and early with a stunning view of the town of *Ullapool* from the top of *Ullapool Hill* at sunrise before you make your way south along *Loch Broom*. Stop off at the unmissable *Corrieshalloch Gorge* to marvel at the tumbling cascade of the *Falls of Measach* and enjoy the view from the viewing platform at the end of the gorge.

As you make your way south, park up at the viewpoint overlooking *Little Loch Broom*, famous for its part in the movie "Shell", with beautiful views of the loch to the east and the open ocean to the west. This region of Wester Ross is mostly comprised of small and cute harbour towns, so make your way south and pay a visit to a few. *Poolewe* and *Gairloch* are the top recommendations.

The last two stops of the day sit on the southern coast of *Loch Maree*, where you can find the beautiful *Victoria Falls* and the fascinating *Beinn Eighe NNR Centre*. At the southern end of the loch lies the small town of Kinlochewe, a fantastic place to rest your head for the night.

76 KYLESKU BRIDGE

Day Five - The fifth and final day of the road trip continues southwest through the *Torridon Pass*, stopping off at the cute town of *Shieldaig*, before moving onto the small town of *Applecross*. If you are a confident driver in a small car then you can reach this via the nailbiting *Bealach na Ba pass*. However, if you have a larger vehicle it can be reached via the picturesque and winding coastal road along the north of the *Applecross Peninsula*.

Either way, the final destination at *Applecross* is worth the journey, sitting at the edge of the mainland and looking across the sea to Skye. Pay a visit to the *Applecross Inn* for a hot meal and possibly some live entertainment, before either staying the night in *Applecross* or beginning the journey back to *Inverness* to round up your NC500 road trip.

112 BEALACH NA BA

41 JOHN O'GROATS SIGNPOST

How to Spend 7 Days on the NC500

Spending an entire week on the northern route allows for a slower and more relaxed pace, with a couple of days spent in locations unique to this part of the world. This is the most popular length of time to explore the North Coast 500.

Day One - The first day of the trip can be spent exploring the city centre of Inverness, soaking up the culture before you begin your journey north to *Dornoch*. Visit the *Inverness Castle* and the *Museum and Art Gallery*, and learn about the history of the region and the different cultures it has been host to over the centuries.

Enjoy a walk along the *River Ness* to the secluded *Ness Islands* and take in the beautiful serenity of nature that can be found not far from the centre of this northern capital. If you want to learn more about the history of the city, tour buses give an excellent overview of Inverness and the surrounding area, a perfect way to get to know the history of Scotland before you begin your road trip.

Before you leave the city, be sure to spend some time exploring the high street and stocking up on souvenirs and essential supplies before you head northwards.

Spend the night here in the city itself or further north in the small town of *Dornoch*. Either way, be sure to explore the local area and enjoy the bars and restaurants that the area has to offer.

Day Two - Start off the day with a luxurious hot chocolate from the *Cocoa Mountain Cafe* in *Dornoch* and stretch your legs on the endless golden sands of *Dornoch Beach*.

Turning your attention west, head inland to witness the natural phenomenon of the leaping salmon at the *Falls of Shin*. Here you can see the spectacular migration of salmon making their way up the insane heights of the waterfalls as they head inland to breed.

Continuing north, the next stop is at the beautiful *Dunrobin Castle*, one of the most picturesque castles in Scotland. Towering over the splendid gardens that sit at the back of the castle, it is possible to either enjoy a guided tour of the interior or simply wander through the gardens and soak up the peace and tranquility there.

The famous *Brora Sands* sits another 25 minutes further north of *Dunrobin Castle* and is well worth a stop. The beautiful, white-sand beaches stretch along the coast for miles and the town is small and quaint. Cows wander around the shoreside golf course and offer the perfect photo opp if you like cute animals.

Our next stop is one of our highlights of the trip, the *Whaligoe Steps*. This staircase has been built into the vertical drop of the Whaligoe slate cliffs and provides a stunning view below. The *Whaligoe Steps* are a series of limestone steps leading down the 250ft cliffside to a sheltered harbour area below.

Just 15 minutes on from Whaligoe, the next stop is at *Castle Wick*. This castle ruin sits on an outcrop of land from the surrounding cliffs, with perilous drops on either side. The *Castle of Old Wick* is believed to date back to the 12th century. However, all that remains today is the towering ruins of the 4-storey tower.

Further on towards the end of the world you'll find the rather impressive remains of *Castle Sinclair and Girnigoe*. This is definitely the most awe-inspiring castle ruin we have ever visited. If you are a Game of Thrones fan you do NOT want to miss this!

35 CASTLE OF OLD WICK

Finish off the day at the northern point of *John O'Groats* and relax in the one of the bars or restaurants with a stunning view of the ocean.

Day Three - Start the day off nice and early with a sunrise view over the incredible sea columns known as the *Duncansby Stacks*. Sitting 60m above the unforgiving swells of the North Sea, these sea stacks are a testiment to the unbelievable power of nature in this ancient part of the world.

From here, head back into *John O'Groats* for a quick photo with the iconic sign post before turning west along the northern coast. Not too far away sits the beautiful stretch of sand known as *Dunnet Bay*, a crescent moon shaped beach that spans some 1000m along the north coast.

Next up, visit the nearby *Castle of Mey* and enjoy a tour of the splendid interior of the castle that dates back to the 16th-century and was a set of the hit Netflix show, The Crown.

42 DUNCANSBY HEAD STACKS

urther along the coast, on the border between Caithness and Sutherland, the small ove known as *Puffin Cove* is a slightly tricky walk from the main road. However, the final estination is worth the effort. *Puffin Cove* is one of the more undiscovered sights on the C500 that is definitely worth a visit.

ounding off the third day on the route, the sliver of land home to the *Strathy Point ighthouse* is a fantastic place to marvel at the sunset on the northern coast. acing directly west, watch as the sun sets into the ocean before heading for your bed for he night, another long day to look forward to tomorrow.

ay Four - If seeing another sunrise is on he cards, the nearby vantage point of *trathy Beach* is the place to view it. Perched igh above the beach itself, the car park elivers incredible views of the bay and the urrounding cliffs.

he road trip continues to head westward owards the northern coast, along winding oads and between towering giants. As you rive along the coastal road, the sea far elow to the right, keep your eyes peeled or the isolated paradise of *Coldbackie each*, hidden from view by the guarding and dunes around it. This beach is one

of the most secluded and beautiful on the route, sitting only a few hundred metres from the main road and yet undiscovered by most. The near vertical path leading down to it puts off most visitors, however, it is actually easier than you think to get down.

Continuing on through the town of *Tongue*, the next stop sits on the horizon to the south, overlooking the Kyle of Tongue. *Castle Varich* sits high atop a hill, proud and defiant against the dramatic backdrop of mountains. The trek to this ruin is short and easy, and the views from the castle of the bay below are simply incredible.

54 COLDBACKIE BEACH

Back onto the road and across the causeway leading away from *Tongue*, the next stop sits in the town of *Durness* and is one of the most fascinating on the trip. The ancient *Smoo Cave* dates back to the time of the Vikings and has been the discovery point of many artifacts suggesting their residence in this cave. Tours run through the cave system and give an incredible insight into the history of this area.

There are a few beaches in this area that are beautiful to behold, from the dramatic cliffs over *Ceannabeine Beach* to the golden *Sango Sands* and *Balnakeil Beach*, these beaches are all a perfect place to relax and enjoy the view. If you are looking for a place to spend the night, the Sango Sands Oasis is an award-winning campsite overlooking the beach.

Day Five - The next day the route turns southwards, leaving behind the north and introducing you to the rugged wilderness of the famous western coast. Explore the winding roads along the northern coast of *Loch Inchard*, towards the town of Kinlochbervie, and wander along the beautiful *Oldshoremore Beach*.

The next stop lies to the south on the very western coast of Sutherland at Tarbet Harbour. Here you can catch a small boat across to the nature reserve of *Handa Island*, a crucial nesting spot for thousands of sea birds that make their way to Scotland each and every year. Explore the island for a couple of hours and make sure you don't miss the boat back to the mainland.

64 SANGO SANDS BEACH

Heading southwards, the award-winning *Kylesku Bridge* bends the road through the seemingly impenetrable horizon of towering peaks and deep lochs, eventually leading you to the beautiful banks of *Loch Assynt*. Here the road turns west towards one of Scotland's most famous and beautiful beaches, *Achmelvich Bay*. The torquoise water and white sand here resemble that of the Caribbean, although the water temperature unfortunately doesn't.

Doubling back towards Loch Assynt, the road passes by the ruins of *Castle Ardvreck*, which sits on a spit of land towards the middle of the loch, and winds its way southwards through the ancient and fascinating landscape where continents collide, the *Knockan Crag Nature Reserve*.

Depending on how much daylight is left, the one-hour hike to the *Allt nan Uamh (Bone Caves)* is definitely an activity that cannot be missed. Visit the ancient caves where the bones of multiple ancient predators were discovered, such as polar bears and wolves.

Continue south through the nature reserve, passing the visitor centre where you can learn about the geology of this landscape, including a discovery that revolutionised the thinking of geologists across the world.

The final stop for the day is in the harbour town of *Ullapool*, the perfect place to end a busy day with warming pubs, delicious restaurants, and a beautiful view of *Loch Broom*.

95 ULLAPOOL

Day Six - Start the day off early with a quick walk up *Ullapool Hill*, where you can enjoy panoramic views of *Loch Broom* and the surrounding landscape. From here, look southwards towards the first stop of the day at the deep and powerful *Corrieshalloch Gorge*, located at the southern end of *Loch Broom*.

The endless cascade of the *Falls of Measach* carves a deep ravine into the land, falling 46m into the *Corrieshalloch Gorge*. The waterfall can be viewed either from the suspension bridge that leads over it, or from the viewing platform at the end of the trail that looks back towards the bridge and waterfall.

From here, continue south along the A832, winding your way between the shoulders of the giants that lie dormant in this part of Scotland and stop off to enjoy the views from some of the harbour towns that sit along the route, such as *Poolewe* and *Gairloch*.

Driving south along *Loch Maree*, the beautiful *Victoria Falls* sits just a short walk from the car park, easily accessible by a flat, dirt path. From here, continue along the banks of *Loch Maree* and stop off at the *Beinn Eighe Visitor Centre* to learn more about the fascinating and diverse wildlife and flora that can be found around the highlands of Scotland.

As the day comes to an end, make the most of the remaining daylight by visiting the viewpoint at Glen Docherty, which looks back down the A832 towards *Kinlochewe* and *Loch Maree*, and then double back towards the town. Either spend the night here or further along the route towards *Torridon*.

Day Seven - On the final day of the route, be sure to take your time as you make your way through the stunning scenery of Wester Ross, along the narrow and winding roads that navigate this region. Along the lower banks of *Loch Torridon* and past *Loch Shieldaig*, the road turns south towards *Lochcarron* and the final stretch of the road trip.

Your journey, however, is far from over as this final day contains one of the most scenic and nailbiting drives yet. By taking either the direct route over the mountainous terrain of the Applecross Peninsula, known as the *Bealach na Ba Pass* or by touring the longer scenic route on the northern coast, *Applecross* is the final destination for this trip.

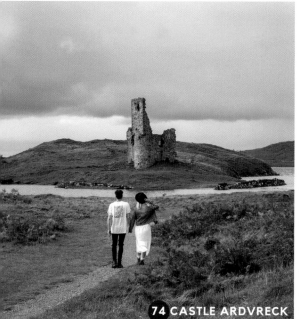

74 CASTLE ARDVRECK

Make your way around this desolate and unforgiving part of the country and take extra care on the narrow, winding, and slightly eroded roads that lead the way. Keep an eye out for wildlife on the northern route, with sheep, highland cows, and even deer inhabiting the area.

Once you reach the town of *Applecross* spend some time exploring the main street and the small shops that can be found along here, or head out to the *Applecross Walled Garden* for a coffee and cake.

Finish the trip off with a night to remember in the cosy and welcoming *Applecross Inn*, offering delicious food, refreshing drinks, and live entertainment.

How to Spend 14 Days
on the NC500

The most relaxed and enjoyable length of time to spend exploring the North Coast 500, fourteen days allows you to take your time on the route with days off from the hectic running around of sightseeing. The itinerary for this 2-week road trip is the same as the 7-day, with the addition of a day on the Black Isle, a day in Easter Ross, and some day trips into the hills to enjoy the scenery that the highlands has to behold. The sights that we recommend in these extra days are listed below, with the choice of which are best for you being entirely up to yourself.

The Black Isle - The Black Isle is a fairly small peninsula north of the Moray Firth that is often overlooked by people exploring the region. Upon visiting the Black Isle, the best sight to see is the *Fairy Glen Falls*, an aptly named set of fairytale-like waterfalls hidden deep in the forest that once covered the entire penisula. Other sights that can't be missed also include *Chanonry Point* for a chance to spot the local marine life, such as dolphins and porpoises, as well as the tranquil beach at *Rosemarkie Bay*. Of course, for any beer enthusiasts, there is also the *Black Isle Brewery*, which offers tours of the UK's first organic brewery.

Easter Ross - Another often overlooked area of the NC500 is the southern end and eastern coast of Easter Ross. Here you will find a number of hidden gems that make for the perfect day out exploring. If you are looking to bag your first NC500 munro, the relatively straight-forward (albeit rather vertical) *Ben Wyvis* offers stunning views of its surroundings. The waterfalls known as *Rogie Falls* and *Black Water Falls* sit not too far from here as well and are both situated along easily accessible paths.

To the east of Tain lie the small, seaside towns of *Portmahomack*, *Shandwick*, and *Balintore*, as well as the *Tarbat Ness Lighthouse* on the most northerly spit of the peninsula.

Caithness - Leaving from the harbour of *John O'Groats*, it is possible to embark on a ferry across to *Burwick, Orkney* for an overnight stay or a couple of days exploring.

If beaches are more your thing, then of course it is possible to spend a day exploring, relaxing and swimming on many of the lesser known stretches of golden sand on the north coast, such as the *Bay of Sannick* by the *Duncansby Lighthouse*, or *Melvich Beach* further west into Sutherland, and the peaceful harbour at *Skerray Bay*.

Northwest Sutherland - Crossing the Kyle of Durness, the Cape Wrath Ferry will take passengers onto the almost inaccessible northern peninsula of *Cape Wrath*, where it is possible to hike to the most northerly bothy in Scotland, the *Kearvaig Bothy*. This walk is a two day activity, with an 8-mile trek across pretty barren land to get to the destination. On the other side of the

Cape Wrath Peninsula, a much easier hike along a firm path will take you 4 miles to one of Scotland's most remote beaches, *Sandwood Bay*.

Further to the south, another notable walk takes you out along the coast of the spit of land where you will find Achmelvich Bay, to the *Lighthouse and Sea Stack of Stoer*. The path from the lighthouse to the *Old Man of Stoer* is rather boggy and difficult to follow, and will take about 3 hours return.

Vearing west from the A835, the small and isolated villages of *Achiltibuie* and *Altandhu* deliver stunning views across the water to the wonderfully named *Summer Isles* on Scotland's western coast. This is a popular spot for sea kayaking and stand-up paddleboarding, with the inner isles being reasonably accessible for experienced sea-goers.

45 DUNNET HEAD LIGHTHOUSE

Index

Sights

Accommodation

Dining

Written:
Gemma Spence
Campbell Kerr

Photos:
Gemma Spence
Campbell Kerr

Editing:
Campbell Kerr

Design:
Campbell Kerr
Gary Fu (Rocktiger Designs)

FSC
www.fsc.org
MIX
Paper from
responsible sources
FSC® C117931

Scan the barcode below for access to the Destination NC500 map, showing all sights listed in this book

SCAN ME

Photo copyrights:

Author Acknowledgements:

Throughout the production of the book itself, as well as the years leading up to its conception, the support of the families and friends of both Gemma and Campbell have been unbelievable. Campbell would like to thank his family for the unquestioning support they have shown not only in this project, but in all of the crazy ideas and passions that he has shown throughout his life. Gemma would like to thank her family and close friends for the continuous support they have shown throughout this project and her many other adventures over the years.

An endless thanks also extends to Gary for the unwavering support and passion that he has shown to this project, offering his advice and services without hesitation to make this book what it is today.

Health, Safety, and Responsibility:

As with any outdoor and adventure activity, from land to water-based, there is always a level of risk with those discussed in this book. The locations in this book are all prone to dangerous conditions caused by nature, floods, droughts, high winds, severe rain, snow, and foggy conditions. While the authors of this book have gone to great lengths to ensure the accuracy of the information provided in this book, they will not be held legally or financially responsible for any accident, injury, loss or inconvenience sustained as a result of the information or advice contained in this guide. All activities that are discussed in this book are done entirely at the reader's own risk.

LIKE ANY PICTURES? GET A CANVAS PRINT

All pictures shown in this guide, as well as many others that were captured along the route, are all available for canvas print for you to enjoy in your home. Visit our website shown below for the full range of prints, or get in touch at the email below for any special requests.

Get in touch - contact@destinationearthguides.com

www.destinationearthguides.com